I HEARD IT THROUGH THE PLAYGROUND

616 Best Tips from the Mommy and Daddy Network for Raising a Happy, Healthy Child from Birth to Age Five

Joel Fram, Carol Boswell, and Margaret Maas, M.D.

HarperPerennial
A Division of HarperCollins*Publishers*

HarperCollins books may be purchased for educational, business, or sales promotional use. For information, please write: Special Markets Department, HarperCollins Publishers, Inc., 10 East 53rd Street, New York, NY 10022.

FIRST EDITION

Designed by Laura Hough

Library of Congress Cataloging-in-Publication Data

Fram, Joel, 1944–
I heard it through the playground : 616 best tips from the mommy and daddy network for raising a happy, healthy child from birth to age five / by Joel Fram, Carol Boswell, and Margaret Maas. — 1st ed.
p. cm.
ISBN 0-06-096898-2
1. Child rearing. 2. Parenting. I. Boswell, Carol, 1945– . II. Maas, Margaret, 1949– . III. Title.
HQ769.B656 1993
649'.1—dc20 92-54855

---

93 94 95 96 97 ❖/ RRD 10 9 8 7 6 5 4 3 2

To Jacob
who has brightened our lives
and made them immeasurably more interesting

J.F. and M.M.

To my inspirations,
Gillian and Jonathan

C.B.

Contents

Contents

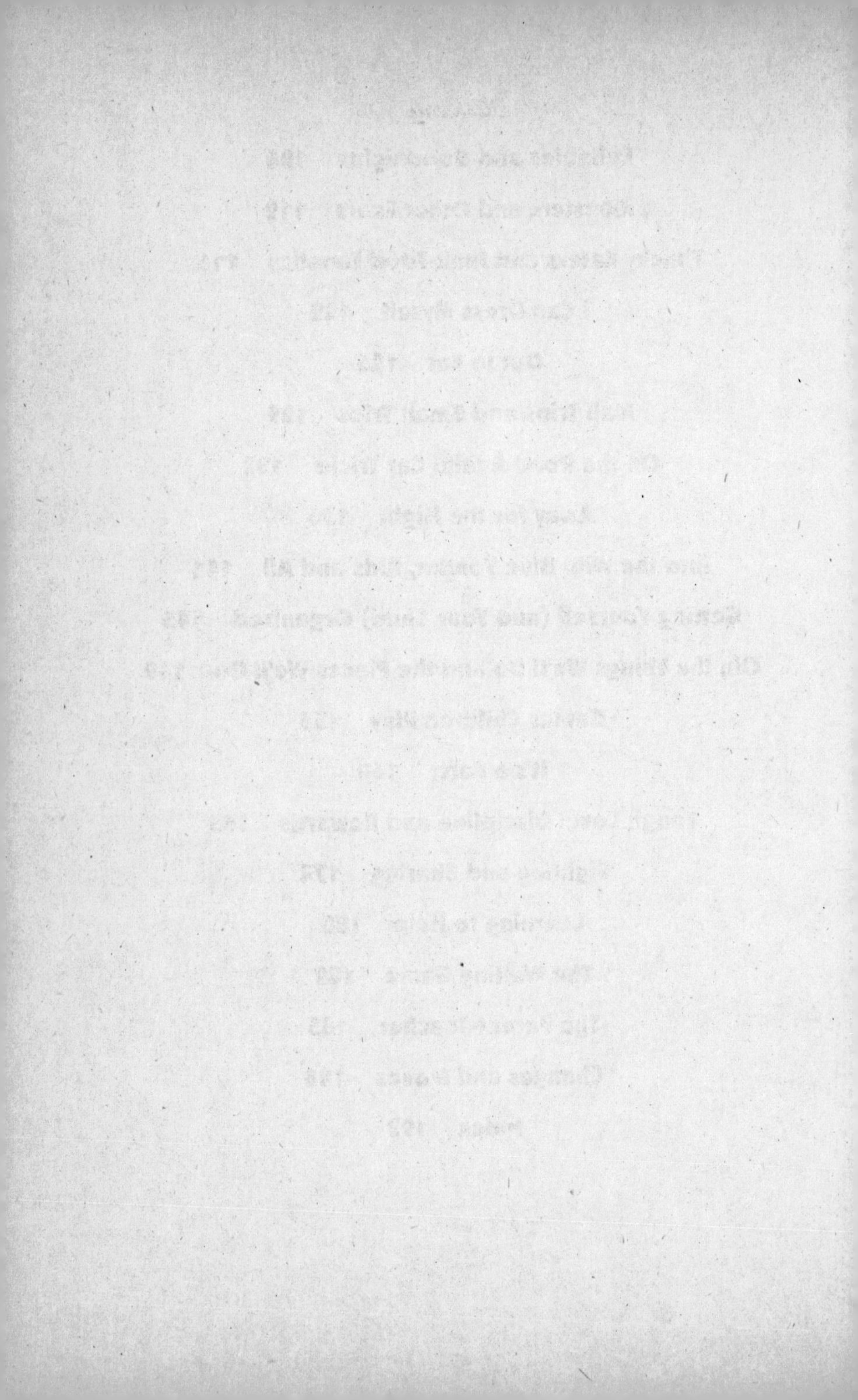

Acknowledgments

This book would not have been possible without the moms and dads across the country who generously shared their useful and innovative tips with us. We would also like to thank the following individuals who helped to create this book: John Boswell, Patty Brown, Ward Calhoun, Janet Kassar, Gail Koff, Matty Kreisberg, Iris Levinson, Liz Mays, and Jane Roth, the wonderful staff of Eeyore's Books for Children, and the owners and staff of Totally for Small People of New Hope, Pennsylvania, who are an inspiration on how to manage a roomful of kids with respect, love, and lots of fun. Finally, special thanks are due to Dale Burg and Richard Nusser, and to our editor, Stephanie Gunning, for giving the book a single, friendly voice.

Introduction

Newborn Jacob had been admired and put into his crib, and the grown-ups had settled down to dinner. The party included the three of us: Joel, Jacob's father and the owner of bookstores for children; Margaret, Jacob's mother and a practicing physician; and Carol, an editor and mother of two children of her own.

As we started on our first course, the baby began to wail. We parents took turns soothing him as we confessed to our guests that we hadn't had a quiet evening—or even a good night's sleep—in weeks. We'd tried everything the experts had to offer but Jacob never settled down until after he'd worn us all out.

"This sounds crazy . . ." began one of the guests, "but at the playground the other day one of the mothers told me she'd found the best way to calm a crying infant. You use the clothes drier."

She laughed at our skeptical expressions. "You don't put the baby *inside* the drier. You put him on *top.* First you lay a diaper pad on the machine, then you put the baby on that. The combination of the movement and the warmth apparently puts the baby out."

Our curiosity piqued, we left the dinner table and headed into the laundry room. Sure enough, within several minutes after he'd been put atop the drier, Jacob's cries diminished. And shortly thereafter he drifted along to dreamland. He was returned to his crib and once again we settled down to dinner—this time, undisturbed.

As we sat over coffee, enjoying the calm, we began to talk about the fact that while there is no shortage of advice from the professionals about how to care for a baby, what is sometimes even more helpful is advice passed from parent to parent—exchanged during nursery-school pickups, over a restaurant table, in the supermarket, or at the playground.

Some of these are a mixed bag of old wives' tales and chance discoveries, techniques without much scientific basis that somehow work almost magically—"like a charm," as the person who passes along the tip is likely to promise.

Others are tidbits of advice that simply aren't covered in the manuals written by professionals: suggestions for packing the diaper bag or restaurant "busy bag," buying the right kind of baby clothes, or packing for a trip.

As book people, we recognized a good book idea when we saw it. We needed only to gather ideas from parents who were willing to sort out and share the best information they had acquired firsthand. Collected in a single volume, these ideas would be a wonderful source of help. Even a single idea or two could mean a major savings of time and energy—resources of which no parent ever has enough.

We canvassed the clientele of Joel's bookstores, solicited tips from parents through nationally circulated publications, and put our heads together to cull suggestions from our own parenting experience. (Of course by the time this book was finished, Joel and Margaret had become old hands at dealing with infants.)

Almost all the advice we received concerned raising children up to about kindergarten age. It appears that the problems of caring for older children become more complex and the solutions more particular, while there is a tremendous amount of similarity among problems of the early years, problems like diapering and dealing with tantrums.

We were delighted (and not really surprised) to find there was no shortage of parents eager to contribute their thoughts and no shortage, either, of ingenious ideas. Out of thousands of solutions, we culled the hundreds of exceptionally good ones that follow.

These aren't theories and they aren't based on laboratory experiments. They are tips that real parents have used in real life while raising real children. We are certain you'll come away with more than a few that you will put to good use . . . and most likely pass along to other parents at the playground.

Joel Fram
Carol Boswell
Margaret Maas, M.D.

What (Else) to Do Before the Baby Comes

Expectant mothers may have plenty to do while they're playing the waiting game—but with a new baby in the house there's even less time. First-time moms are often amazed at how difficult it can be to snatch a few minutes for the most ordinary things—like taking a nice warm bath. Do as much as you can ahead of time so life will be more relaxed when your baby arrives.

Fresh start Before your baby is due, hire a cleaning person to come in and give your house a thorough cleaning. You'll be out of commission for a while but at least the house will stay relatively clean until you have the strength to tackle it yourself.

Packing list Don't forget these for your hospital stay: toothbrush, toothpaste; comb and brush; blow drier; makeup mirror;

address book (dad can use this to make calls announcing the arrival); stationery for notes; pen; notebook to jot down questions, thoughts, things to buy, names of people who send flowers and cards; books about babies and nursing; pillow and plastic cover from home; pretty robe and slips, nursing gown; camera and VCR plus film; comfortable outfit for you to come home in; and receiving blanket (plus hat and sweater in cool weather) to dress the baby for homecoming.

Ready to go Don't wait until the pains are coming one minute apart to gather what you'll need. Have the hospital bag ready at least two weeks ahead of the due date.

Baby doctor Although some books suggest interviewing a pediatrician before your baby is born, often you aren't sure what questions to ask and the interview becomes pointless: only when you actually deal with the doctor do you know whether or not his or her style is compatible with yours. If you're not comfortable with the doctor you start with, find another. Get recommendations from friends. Or ask your obstetrician, who knows your personality and should be able to find a doctor who's a match. Or ask the opinion of residents in a local teaching hospital: they observe all the doctors in action.

Mom's network Before the baby has come (or after, of course), try to join or form a group of new mothers to share ideas. Put up a note at the obstetrician's or pediatrician's office asking if a group exists or if anyone is interested in starting one. Or find people through your Lamaze instructor or hospital. This is how you get your best information.

Class reunions We're not talking about high school or college reunions, we're talking about a get-together with parents from your Lamaze class. Staying in touch is one of the best ways to plug into your local mommy-and-daddy network and get advice from people who've Been There—or Are There. So take down all the names of classmates before the big day. Then, before your baby is two months old, plan a reunion at your house or offer to help another mother with the preparations if she has more room to host the get-together. Both mothers and fathers will enjoy exchanging information. This is the place to start looking for baby-sitters, making friends, and meeting future playmates for your child.

Freebies for babies Expectant or new mothers who call those 800 numbers in the back of baby magazines will be rewarded with freebies, samples, and coupons from many stores and manufacturers. If you don't mind putting up with occasional telephone sales calls, you can double your freebie allowance by listing the addresses of your mother and mother-in-law as well.

Rebate endowment Don't miss out on opportunities for "found money" that can be stashed away for your new child's college fund. You can start building it before the baby comes. Many manufacturers offer rebates on both small and major purchases (cars, appliances). If you qualify, send the required form in under your child's name so that the rebate check can be deposited directly into his account.

Trial run Have your husband clock the amount of time it takes to get to the hospital, and investigate the best routes to take for different times of the day. What's a speedy run at 10 A.M. may be a crawl at the rush hour. And when you're in labor, you don't want to wait one extra second.

Postpartum impression When buying new clothes to wear after the baby comes, you'll be looking forward to looking like your old self. But your style may have to change slightly. Get rid of your hoop earrings, breakable necklaces, etc., since baby will reach for them. Also get things that are loose, dark, and have pockets. They should also be washable. When the baby presses up against you with yogurt mouth . . . yuck.

History in the making We've put this tip in prearrival planning because if it isn't planned it might be too late (or inconvenient) to follow through. The day your baby arrives, make sure someone has bought a copy of several leading newspapers—local, national, and maybe even international. Put aside a couple of newsmagazines, too. Save them all for your baby's scrapbook—or twenty-first birthday. For extra fun, tape the nightly news on the birth day and you'll have a personalized time capsule that will awaken memories in years to come.

Gearing Up: The Nursery and Layette

Aside from the purely decorative decisions (what wallpaper pattern or paint color?), there are many practical ones to be made when you plan the nursery. And there's a lot of equipment to buy that may be unfamiliar to you. Fortunately, many of your decisions can be made as you go along or—if you change your mind—adapted to the needs of you and your baby. But, benefiting from hindsight, moms have passed along some suggestions that may not have occurred to you.

Layette-in-waiting Some mothers don't like to buy layettes until they bring healthy babies home from the hospital. But since it's unlikely you'll be able to go out and shop soon after the birth, go to the local baby-supply store and select what you want, confer with the salespeople, and have the whole list ready so it can be called in and picked up at the appropriate time. It should include cloth diapers, receiving blankets, kimonos, and diapers as well as crib bumpers and sheets.

Brighten up You may have chosen pastels for the nursery decor, but babies prefer, and are stimulated by, bright colors. So add some bright touches when you select a mobile and crib toys.

When the lights go down low Installing a simple dimmer switch at the entrance to your child's room lets you control overhead lights so that you don't completely awaken a half-asleep child with the glare of full illumination. The dimmer gives you just enough light for middle-of-the-night bed checks and feeding and provides "Just a little light, please" that will calm night-time fears when your child is older.

Fan mail So many parents recommended the calming effects of ceiling fans in the nursery we wish we owned a ceiling-fan factory. Summer, winter, spring, or fall, the gentle motion of a ceiling fan does more than circulate hot air or cool air. Its steady hum is also a mesmerizing device for lulling little ones to sleep.

Any old rocker won't do A rocking chair in the nursery is a treat for mom and baby (fathers love it, too). You're off your rocker, though, if you don't get one with arms to hold your elbows and the baby's weight. No matter how pretty, a rocker without arms is useless in the nursery.

Riding in style Although large, traditional baby carriages are beautiful and may have been part of your image of parenthood since you first read Mary Poppins, they are actually impractical. The baby will use it for only a brief period and it's hard to transport. You're better off with a small carriage–car seat combination (see the following hint) plus the lightest-weight stroller you can find. (Some of them are designed to carry even the smallest infants.)

Crib substitute You don't have to rush out and buy a crib right away. Some parents have found it more convenient to keep the baby in a small carriage in their room for the first few weeks. The baby feels comfortable, is easily rocked, and can be moved from room to room with you without being disturbed. A carriage that separates from the base and doubles as a car seat–traveling bassinet is the most practical. You can take the baby everywhere—to friends' homes, to restaurants, and on weekend trips.

Mirror, mirror Outside of the Wicked Queen, no one likes to look in the mirror as much as a baby. Plastic mirrors attached to the crib will amuse and distract your child for many minutes. But never use glass mirrors.

Wheel life When you're buying a stroller, get one that has brakes, front wheels that swivel, and handlebars of a good height. There are handlebars that can be attached to some models to make them higher.

Keeping posted A bulletin board in a small baby's room is helpful for posting medical information, sticking up a barrette or a single sock, putting up birthday cards, etc. As the child grows, she will make her own decisions about what should be put on display.

Time for a change Equip the changing table with diapers (and pins or clips, if you're using cloth diapers), washcloth, cotton balls, change of clothes, baby wipes, bowl for water, and toys to amuse the baby while you work.

Sheeting substitutes Pillowcases are fine sheets for bassinets.

Lid on it When you're buying those cute little furry animals and adorable little picture frames, don't forget the practical items. A large diaper pail—with cover—is a must for the nursery. Even if you're using disposables, you'll need a place to chuck the soiled diaper while hands are kept busy putting on a new one.

At the Hospital

If this is your first hospital stay, you may be anxious about it, but the experience of being in the maternity ward is very different from any other hospital confinement. Chances are you will see a great deal more of the nurses than of your doctor, and at this point they are wonderful sources of advice, because they are thoroughly knowledgeable about infants—and about the fears of first-time moms.

Staff privileges The quality of nursing care makes the difference between a pleasant hospital stay and a feeling of let-me-out-of-here; also, a good nurse can help you become accustomed to your baby and its care much more efficiently. To show the nursing staff that they're appreciated (and, let's be honest, to inspire a feeling of good will), it's thoughtful of your husband, mom, or other close relative to bring a platter of cookies, flowers, or some other small gift to be placed at the nursing desk.

Class act Classes for new moms in the hospital can help you with bathing, wrapping, feeding. If the nurse forgets to mention these, ask her about them.

Postnatal bonus Before you leave the maternity ward with your new baby, ask a nurse if you can get free samples of formula or glucose water. Hospital brands often have longer expiration dates than store-bought ones and the samples are useful whether you're breast-feeding or not. Once the question of samples is raised, very often a busy nurse will remember that other freebies—often special "new mom" kits—are available as well.

Going-away kid Certain items used for your baby's care can be taken home from the hospital. Ask if you can have a nasal syringe, baby's brush or comb, and thermometer.

Pressure relievers If you've had an episiotomy, the nurse may suggest certain comforts both in the recovery room and several days later. These include an inner tube or a foam-rubber pillow to sit on (ask if you can take it home from the hospital) and the use of any or all of the following: premoistened pads, a heat lamp, local anesthetic, ice pack (sometimes the hospital staff use a rubber glove with crushed ice and water).

And Baby Makes Three: Rescheduling Your Life

If this is your first baby, your life will be turned completely upside down, for now you have someone depending on you all the time. Your time is not your own—and neither is it your spouse's, which is why many marriages get a little rocky in the months after the birth, when the excitement has died down a little and the routine (and sleeplessness) may get to you. Recognize that every new set of parents feels as discombobulated as you do, share these feelings with others, ask for advice, and remember that things eventually do start to feel normal again.

Working with the clock The first baby will change your life completely—but it's important to spend some time alone with your spouse. Trying to find that time requires imagination and thinking ahead. If you know you're going to have a busy day ahead of you and will appreciate some time with your spouse, wake the baby up earlier that morning, and cut his afternoon nap, so he'll go to sleep earlier that evening. If you need more time in the morning, reverse the process, and put him down later the night before.

Finding spare time Just because you have a new baby doesn't mean you have to change your lifestyle entirely. If Friday night was your regular night out, continue the custom—and take the baby along. Unless you're used to discoing the night away or driving Grand Prix racing cars, you can enjoy your routine outings—to dinner, a museum, or a movie, provided the movie is not a crash-and-burn feature with a high-decibel sound track. Just plan ahead a little (for example, find out if the museum permits strollers). An adventure is good for all three of you. As the child gets older, venturing forth into the "adult world" will be second nature to him. And when other parents' kids are whining and clinging, yours will be enjoying himself with you.

Double time Putting baby to sleep and vacuuming your house at the same time is a cinch if you put the child in a Snugli. Babies like to see the back-and-forth rocking motion mommy makes, and the sound of the machine is like white noise. Caution: with some babies, the sound has the opposite effect and may set off a wail. Experiment.

Sharing responsibilities Mothers and fathers sometimes have different expectations of one another. Fathers say that they are at a loss when told, "You are not helping enough." They would prefer to be asked to do specific tasks. Mothers have to learn to ask for help (which will usually be given) rather than wait for it (and be resentful if it is not offered). They also have to learn that while dad's style of doing things may be different, it is not necessarily wrong.

Spring ahead, fall behind When daylight savings time starts in the fall, parents can steal an extra hour's sleep or quiet time by *not* switching their baby's schedule. Leave the clock in your baby's room set to standard time to remind you of this. Of course, the baby will make up that extra hour by staying up later—but maybe you'd prefer his company in the early evening.

Stop, think—then go Plan long car trips around your baby's nap and bedtime with a stop in between for dinner and play.

Room service You will want to carry your baby around with you as you go from room to room, but you may need to find time to get your work done. Have a different "activity" set up in each room—a swing in the den, an infant seat in the bedroom, a blanket with toys in the living room, a Johnny Jump-up in the kitchen. As you carry the baby from room to room, there's a new distraction.

Let baby call the shots Sometimes the baby just needs your undivided, unpressured attention. If the day isn't going right and the baby is off the schedule you have set, try conforming to the one she is setting for herself. Allow as much playtime, nursing time, etc. as baby demands. You'll both relax.

Setting a pattern Children like routines, so encourage ones that you find helpful—for example, putting the child down for a nap after lunch every day. (This won't work on all babies—some don't need the sleep, but it may work on yours.)

Big Brother/Big Sister: Mixed Emotions

Big brothers and sisters ought to share in the excitement of the new baby's arrival, but they're sometimes lost in the shuffle—and the lack of attention can be frustrating to them. Preparing them for the arrival of the new baby in as many ways as possible is helpful. So offer an explanation that the baby is coming not because the other child or children aren't satisfactory but—on the contrary—because he or they are so delightful that mommy and daddy want more. Understanding relatives and friends can help make siblings feel important, but the best reassurance that they still occupy a special place in their parents' hearts comes from mom and dad themselves. The better job you do of this, the better the chance that (after the inevitable childhood quarrels), the siblings will learn to love one another for a lifetime.

From the heart Take the sibling to the obstetrician with you and let him or her listen to the heartbeat of the new baby before its arrival. There'll be an early connection to the newcomer.

Anticipating the arrival Some hospitals offer sibling preparation courses as part of their prenatal service. Children see a movie about what to expect when the new baby arrives, what mommy *must* do, how big brother and sister can help. The children practice diapering a doll, and have the chance to express their own thoughts (including fears and complaints) on the subject.

Changing the focus One way to prepare an about-to-be sibling for the arrival of a new baby is to engage the older child in some of the preparations. Paste a picture of him or her in the middle of a piece of paper or poster board, write "Big Sister (Brother)" and the child's name. Then give the child a set of markers, stickers, and stars—you may want to buy some art supplies especially for this project—and ask that he or she draw a border for the picture. Have the child bring the picture to the hospital to place in the baby's bassinet as a welcoming gift, and bring it home to put up prominently in the nursery.

Demonstration model Get a doll for younger siblings—but you'll be playing with it, not them. The idea is to conduct learning play so the new baby's arrival won't seem threatening. "Let's pretend new baby is hungry. What will it do? Laugh or cry? And when it cries, what does mommy have to do? Pick it up! Like this . . . and feed it, like this . . . and then . . ." Or give your child an infant of her or his own, complete with clothing, diaper, and baby bottle, that arrives home along with mom and the new baby. When the real baby needs a bottle, bring out the doll, too.

Family portraits Bring a picture of an older sibling and tape it to the baby's crib so when the older child comes to visit the hospital it'll be right there. Also have dad take a picture of big brother or sister with the new baby at the hospital. The older one will feel proud of your confidence at allowing him to hold the new baby carefully in his lap and will feel literally in the picture in the new enlarged family.

Something special Have a gift ready for older siblings as soon as the new baby arrives—the sooner the better. If the siblings visit the hospital, give it then rather than waiting until you and the newborn get home. If it happens to be something your older child has wanted for the last three or four months, all the better. Buy it to set aside and hold for the big day. It'll mean more. And by all means, have the gift come from the new baby to help assuage those feelings of jealousy.

Private homecoming If older children will want your immediate attention before the new baby is through the front door, give some thought to having them *out* of the house until mother and baby are settled. When the baby's in the crib or bassinet and everyone's calm and collected, the time is right for renewing not-so-old acquaintances.

Mommy loves you Whenever, or wherever, your other children are going to meet the new baby brother or sister for the first time, let daddy be cradling the newcomer. Then mommy's arms are free to enfold the other children in a loving hug that reminds them you're still there for them.

Equal time If there's a new baby in the house, have some snacks on hand for the older kids when it's feeding time for the newcomer. Keep everyone in the act and you'll have a longer, happier run.

Benefits of seniority Now that there's a new addition to the family, make sure the older sibling gets some special privileges—the chance to pour her own juice, stay up fifteen minutes later, or even have a desk or work table of her own, now that she has seniority.

Letting it all hang out Toddlers' emotions may be expressed inappropriately at times, but they're valid emotions all the same. Addressing them is important. When the new baby comes home, it's wise to let older siblings know *everyone's* a little on edge when the baby cries, wakes up in the middle of the night, or constantly demands attention (and gets it promptly). Mommy and daddy can acknowledge that caring for a baby can be hard on everyone sometimes, but be reassuring about the fact that patient effort and lots of love on everyone's part will eventually produce a great little brother or sister who will even be fun to play with.

Just mommy and me When sibling rivalry first evidences itself, it's time for some one-on-one with the older child. Leave your baby at home with daddy or baby-sitter while the two of you do something special—a movie, a museum, a puppet show, or a visit to the amusement park. Do it more than once, especially during the first few months after baby's arrival.

Mom's helper The older child will feel important and not resent the newcomer so much if made to feel competent by being asked to handle tasks like bringing the diapers for mom and the bottle for the baby and helping burp the baby.

A kid's best friend A small caged animal such as a hamster is a perfect distraction for a new older sibling. Toddler friends won't care about the baby but they'll fuss over the pet and make the sibling feel special.

Passing out cigars Dad probably won't give out smokes these days, but there's no reason big brother and big sister can't distribute bubble-gum cigars that come in pink or blue. A picture of the newborn can also go to school for show and tell—and the actual baby can be brought along for showing off several months in the future.

Something for the big brother or sister Keep a few wrapped small presents to give your older child when people come bearing gifts for the new baby. Close friends can be asked to make a point of paying some attention to the sibling (congratulations are of course in order) and also refrain from fawning too much over the new arrival.

On guard Keep an eye on the older sibling during the first days and weeks. Anger and jealousy are perfectly normal feelings under these circumstances, but they shouldn't come out in aggressive behavior. One mom covered the bassinet with netting while her baby was sleeping, telling his big brother it was there to ward off mosquitoes. In fact, it was there to prevent blocks and other items from "accidentally" falling on the baby's head.

Hiring the Baby Nurse

Some people are concerned that the presence of a stranger will be too unsettling and choose not to have a baby nurse. But unless you have a close relative who will be with you for the first few days—and unless that close relative has some recent experience with newborns—the arguments for getting help are quite compelling. You may be tired (particularly if you've had a Caesarean section) but, more important if you're a first-time mom, you will appreciate having someone right at hand to answer the many anxious questions you will have in the first few days. It's also nice for new parents to snatch a few moments with the other children and/or just for themselves—if only to go out for a cup of coffee—and a baby nurse can cover in your absence. If you don't know where to get help, visit several of your local playgrounds while you're still pregnant and talk to mothers who've been down the road before. They might supply you with names; so might your pediatrician.

Job description Try to sort out your own priorities before you hire the nurse. Do you want someone who will help you with the baby or someone to help you with the house? A first-time mother will probably want someone to show her fundamentals about baby care while someone more experienced may prefer to handle the baby herself and have help for housekeeping and cooking. In this case, you might prefer to hire a home helper rather than a baby nurse. Do you prefer to be the primary caretaker and want the nurse there just to spell you when you need sleep? Do you want a quiet person to stay in the background or a lively, chatty type? During the interview try to judge the person according to your particular needs.

Checking up, checking out Nothing is better than "word-of-mouth" recommendations when it comes to finding the right nanny or baby-sitter for your child. Even then, it's wise to double-check references. Having the prospective nanny fill out a simple application in front of you during an interview is a good way to check literacy, accuracy, and "grace under pressure." Ask if the applicant has any child-care training or CPR skills, and if she would be willing to attend such courses. If you're hiring someone to care for an infant, ask if she's ever cared for an infant before and if she has done so recently. Many routine infant-care procedures are quickly forgotten; if you decide to hire this particular candidate, make sure you go through them with her.

Emergency drills Make sure you and the baby-sitter have matching lists of emergency phone numbers—doctors, police, fire departments, poison control center, your number at work, neighbors or relatives to call. In addition to posting these numbers in a conspicuous spot in the home, give her a copy to keep in a plastic case in the diaper bag, which will probably be with her at all times. Go over procedures to follow if she loses her keys, feels ill, or has a question that needs an immediate answer in your absence. Decide beforehand (and after consulting with your pediatrician) which hospital you'd prefer her to go to if an emergency-room visit is ever in order, and make sure she knows how to get there.

Making notes When you have a child who's not yet able to speak, you have no way of knowing how the day went. Here's how to keep track of baby *and* the baby-sitter to relieve your anxieties. Have the sitter keep a journal of the day's activities you think are important. How long did baby nap? How's baby's appetite? Mood? Bowel movements? The sitter can mark down her own observations in the book and also note down telephone messages or questions she may have for you about her or baby's routine. Some sitters who may be overwhelmed by the idea of a "journal" may prefer to start out with a questionnaire prepared by you that has some simple structure.

Checking up If you have the slightest suspicion that the nanny isn't up to par, don't always give her the benefit of the doubt—save *that* consideration for yourself and your child. On the other hand, don't panic or start imagining the worst. Have a friend or neighbor drop in occasionally, and unexpectedly, to see how the nanny is getting along with your child if you have any doubts.

Letting go If you want to get rid of the nurse or sitter, you may find the actual firing very difficult to handle. Rather than say that she doesn't measure up, you may wish to find some tactful "out"—for example, "My mother has decided she will come to stay," "My husband is getting a leave from work," or "A relative will be living here as an au pair."

Of Breasts and Bottles

Many of your questions about breast- versus bottle-feeding can be answered by the nurses in the hospital, who will probably be there when you and your infant try this out together. Your pediatrician can also provide additional advice, but other moms who've experienced the problems and pleasures of breast-feeding are the very best source of information. Even if you decide to nurse, at some point down the road you may be dealing with bottles—so here's the best of what moms have to say on both topics.

Double time Older siblings will benefit from the time mom spends nursing the baby if she uses that time as story hour. The pleasant hum of mom's voice will be soothing to the nursing baby, and mom will probably appreciate the chance to spend quiet time with all the children together.

Soothing sounds A cassette of lullaby songs is pleasant both for the baby and for mom when she's nursing in the middle of the night.

Keeping track Rather than transferring a safety pin from one side of the bra to the other to keep track of which breast baby should nurse from first, switch a ring from one hand to the other. It's easier than trying to unclip a pin in the middle of the night. You can also redo the flaps of the bra strap so that one breast is on the first hook and the other on the second, so you know which one to start with.

Sack them Nursing pads can be machine washed—and easily found again—if you put them in one of the drawstring bags meant for lingerie.

Double time Older siblings always seem to need you just at the moment you are starting to nurse the baby. If you take care of the needs of big brother or sister first—by offering food or drink, or settling the child down with an activity—you might be allowed a few moments of quiet.

Alone together Finding a clean, quiet place to breast-feed isn't always easy when you're out shopping. Restrooms may be crowded or unclean, and there may be no place to sit down. Dressing or try-on rooms in clothing stores are a better alternative in stores where space isn't at a premium—or a bathing-suit sale isn't in progress.

Nursing accessories Bright-colored plastic or wood beads on a necklace are a nice complement to a nursing mother's wardrobe, because babies like to look at and touch them. The most practical (since these often break) is a necklace you make yourself. Any old beads, ribbons, etc. will do. One mother fashioned hers from string and a half-dozen colored plastic clothespins that her baby just loved. Substituting elastic for string makes the necklace more likely to stand up to a baby's tugs.

Holding pattern Give a baby a soft cloth diaper to hold every time you nurse or give a bottle. This will train your baby to use it instead of a blanket, and it's better for you because it's smaller, replaceable, and washable. Encourage some sort of "blankey" because it is wonderfully helpful to quiet a child in a variety of new situations or help him settle down to sleep. If your child has chosen something other than a diaper, try to buy at least one duplicate of the item so you've got a substitute in case of an emergency, and launder it regularly to keep it in approximately the same condition as the first.

Warm 'n' quick To heat formula fast, prepare the concentrate in a bottle. Then add warm water and shake. If you overheat it, add a little extra formula that you've stored in a sterile container in the fridge for just this purpose.

Bottle holder To keep bottles from tipping over, save the soda-pop tray from a fast-food restaurant. Bottles fit in perfectly and never spill.

Bottle cooler Fill a bottle with a few ounces of water, cap it, and put it in the freezer. Before you go out, add juice or water. The ice will melt slowly and the bottle stays cold. Parents can enjoy a cool drink too if they try this same technique using a plastic soda or water bottle.

Cool and carry To avoid carrying a large ice chest with a single prepared baby bottle, toss a few ice cubes into a wide-mouthed insulated thermos and drop a bottle inside. The thermos opening measures three inches across and the unbreakable holder measures eleven inches in length. It's perfect for regular bottles or wider disposables. Fits in the diaper bag or can be carried by the thermos handle.

Sipping lessons Teaching a baby to drink from a straw before taking a trip makes it easier to quench his thirst in a restaurant or at the beach and in any other situation when you may not have a bottle handy. Put a straw into a small amount of liquid, hold your finger on top to trap the liquid, and allow the baby to suck on the straw when you release your finger. After one or two tries, even a baby as young as six or seven months will get the idea.

Get a grip When the baby is learning to hold a bottle but her tiny hands can't grip it well, slip a tube sock over the bottle. It'll be much easier to hold.

Bagged and ready For traveling with a formula-fed baby, package the required number of scoops of powdered formula in individual plastic nurser bags and fasten with twist ties. Fill bottles with the correct amount of preboiled water and mix when needed. This ensures that the formula won't spoil, and it sure beats carrying along a cooler.

Rice 'n' easy To clean corners in curved baby bottles that brushes don't quite reach, add uncooked rice and some water, and shake well. The abrasive action of the hard rice loosens the dirt.

Quiet hours If your child wakes in the middle of the night for a bottle, keep the noise and activity level low. Don't make the proceedings entertaining, don't use it as an occasion for an extra cuddle. If the child becomes too wakeful, she'll have trouble going back to sleep and the routine may become more protracted every night. Just do what needs to be done—without turning on the lights (that's why we recommend a dimmer switch)—and then all of you can go back to sleep.

Warming trend When you take your baby from the crib or cradle for a midnight feeding on a cool night, place a heating pad in the empty crib until feeding is over. Remove the pad after feeding, of course, and put baby down onto a nice, warm, cozy spot.

When Baby Can't Sleep

Some babies sleep a lot—and they're the envy of moms whose infants are especially wakeful. Which type of child you have seems to be a matter of genetics. There are, however, some parental tricks to help lull a child to sleep and to soothe him should he awaken. There is some scientific speculation that a baby's cry is designed to be especially distressing in order to ensure that attention will be paid. Mother Nature did a very effective job.

House tour Even the fussiest babies and toddlers often drift off to sleep soon after they're gliding along in a car seat or stroller, but it's not always convenient to make a special outing just for this purpose. Instead of a fuel-burning car ride to nowhere or a stroll around the block in hot, muggy weather, push the baby around the house to produce the desired effect. Maintain an even pace, as if you were outside. If you must pause for a moment, keep the stroller moving back and forth smoothly. Don't jiggle the stroller or jerk it back and forth.

The nearness of you If your baby won't stop crying and you're unable to get any work done, slip her into a Snugli or some other infant carrier and just do what you can under the circumstances. Your hands, at least, are free to make phone calls, perform light work, or get dinner ready.

Lights . . . on There's no reason to turn off all the lights in the house at your baby's bedtime. When he's tired, he'll fall asleep no matter what! There are some children who seem to have night and day confused, and they may need an external clue—like dimmed lights—to encourage them to nod off. But most do not. It's better not to accustom them to pitch darkness and absolute silence so they'll have less trouble at times, such as when you're visiting, when it can't be arranged. The parents of babies who don't get used to the sound of conversation, television, or music filtering through their dreams are still tiptoeing when the babies are well out of diapers.

The shirt off mom's back Your child may be particularly fussy—with a slight cold or an ear infection—but if you rock her all night long, you'll be too exhausted to cope with her tomorrow. Sometimes a garment mom has been wearing—her T-shirt or nightgown—placed under your baby in the crib will be enough to keep her comforted and quiet—quiet enough to drift off to sleep.

Fan-tastic Folks down South used to sit on front porches, rocking their babies in gliders or chairs, waving a fan with their free hands to create a cool breeze and to keep the 'skeeters away. Babies love the soft, repetitive swoosh of a fan, and its mesmerizing movement is very relaxing. They still sell hand fans in novelty stores, but you can make (and even decorate) your own with a piece of shirt cardboard. One mother discovered the calming effect of fans when she used a magazine to fan, and calm, her infant while he was having his portrait taken in a photo studio.

Water babies Put an ear to a stethoscope on an expectant mother's tummy and you'll discover that the gentle movement of intrauterine fluid has a lot in common with the rhythms of ocean waves and water tumbling in rocky brooks—all, as it happens, sleep-inducing sounds. If you don't have access to a brook or ocean, try rocking a fussy baby to sleep by putting her bassinet, stroller, or carriage next to a dishwasher or washing machine in use. Sound-wise, she'll think she's in familiar territory. You can also tape the sound of either appliance's water cycle for replay at crib side.

White noise A baby who is a light sleeper may require some noise—white noise—to help lull him to sleep. And white noise also produces remarkable results after a period of intense crying.

- A humidifier can be effective as a white-noise generator.
- You can also turn on the hair drier or the TV, or tune the radio to a station that has nothing but static.
- Or use a metronome for a wonderfully monotonous sound at bedtime, especially ones that can be timed for extended periods, say up to thirty minutes.
- Or take your baby into the kitchen where the range hood fan is set at the highest speed.
- Or purchase Sleeptite, a commercially available device that cushions baby while producing a gentle vibration and white noise. Information about Sleeptite is available by calling 1-800-NO-COLIC.

- Or tape-record your dishwasher or drier, the sounds of rushing water, or your vacuum cleaner. It will help take the baby's mind off the sometimes startling sounds of the outside world.

Fan dancer A gently spinning ceiling fan has lulled many a child to sleep, but some babies soon get bored with this trick. For a change of pace and a spot of mesmerizing color, tie a light scarf or two onto the blades—small ones that won't get caught in the blades or hang down where your baby can reach them.

Quiet as a lamb One of the most frequently recommended hints we've received for helping babies relax—especially good for newborns—is to purchase a genuine lambskin to place under the baby in the crib. Their soothing effect is universal and some call it miraculous. Many hospitals now use them in infant intensive care units. Lambskins are washable, preferably in a cold-water detergent.

Good vibrations When your baby just won't settle down, put a changing pad—or your lambskin—*and* the baby on top of the drier and turn it on. The combination of the warmth and vibration should knock him right out. Watch carefully that the movement of the machine doesn't move the baby dangerously close to the side.

Bottle helper If you're using a bottle instead of breast-feeding, when your baby is a month old try adding a tablespoon of cereal to the formula with the 10 P.M. feeding. Though you may not get the experts to confirm that there is a scientific basis for this, moms say that the addition of the heavier food seems to help put a baby back to sleep. Check with your pediatrician first.

Sleep stages If the baby you've spent half an hour rocking to sleep in your arms "wakes up" when you first put him down in the crib, it's because he hasn't entered his deep sleep phase. During the first twenty minutes or so of light sleep a baby's eyelids will flutter, fists will remain partially clenched, and muscles will not be completely relaxed. In deep sleep, eyelids are shut tightly and limbs hang loose. Now you know the sandman has arrived and baby's ready to be put down.

Cozy comfort When the baby is placed in the crib, put her head against the bumpers. She will feel more comforted. Littlest babies like being swaddled, too. Let the nurse show you how if you haven't figured it out.

Midnight Crier: The Fussy Baby

Penelope Leach describes the syndrome that she says is best called "evening colic." After the late-afternoon or evening feeding, the baby won't settle down. Though he may sleep briefly, he wakes up and pulls up his knees, screws up his face, and seems to be having terrible stomach pain. Such crying attacks recur. Any newborn may show these symptoms, but infants over two weeks old who continue to cry like this on a regular basis are usually called colicky. The facts (and cures) for this symptom are all hotly debated, but one fact remains: parents are always desperate for solutions to calm a baby suffering from evening colic or crying without any apparent cause such as hunger or the need to be changed. Here are some playground tips to help you out when your baby is particularly fussy, along with a few words of reassurance: the worst period of baby's fretfulness (and colic itself) lasts only about three months.

Colic hold For colicky babies, the "football hold" is a must. With your elbow bent at a ninety-degree angle, cup the child's head in your hand, with her face to the side. Your forearm supports the length of the child's body (stomach down), and arms and legs dangle down the sides of your arm.

- Or hold the baby as you normally would and try to simulate an up-and-down, side-to-side movement that mimics the floating sensation of being in the womb.

Crisis? Maybe not New parents sometimes have a hard time deciding (usually around 3 A.M.) whether or not baby's distress warrants a call to the pediatrician. If you're reluctant to call your doctor, call the maternity unit or nursery at the hospital where you gave birth. You can be sure the nurses are awake, and unless *they're* in the middle of a crisis, nine times out of ten they'll be happy to advise you or calm your worst fears. On the other hand, some parents swear by child-care expert Penelope Leach (*Your Baby from Birth to Age Five*) and her uncanny ability to explain precisely the noncrisis you're experiencing and give you lots of remedies. One mother wrote: "I'd grab the baby and start describing symptoms out loud while my husband ran for her book. It's laid out so well and is so comprehensive that we could easily find a description that described our 'crisis' in detail, and her practical, reassuring comments rang so true she sometimes left us smiling with relief." Other parents swear by Dr. Spock or T. Berry Brazelton.

Dip tip Maybe it's a reminder of what the amniotic fluid feels like, but more than one mother claims this is the greatest for calming a colicky baby—merely dip baby's feet in warm water for a minute.

Double dip If putting baby's feet in the water isn't enough, maybe it's time for you *and* baby to slip into a warm bath *together*. It should calm you both down.

Late-night pacifier Finding a pacifier amidst the bedclothes in the middle of the night is frustrating for parent and infant. So keep a couple of clean ones at hand on the bureau in case baby cries out in the night. For an older child who is still using a pacifier—and we know many who use them until age four—you may put an extra couple of pacifiers right in the bed. Though one may be tangled in sheets or fall onto the floor, if another is at hand the child may pop it into her mouth and go back to sleep without disturbing you.

What's the diagnosis Don't assume your child's distressful bouts of crying are "just colic." Has your pediatrician ruled out milk and formula allergies, among other things, in his diagnosis?

White walls When you hold or rock a colicky infant, face a blank white wall or window shade. This helps reduce the visual stimulation to which colicky babies are overly sensitive.

The Crib and How to Use It

Tiny baby clothes don't make up the bulk of the laundry your small child will create—the bed linens will. Making the crib comfortable, making it fresh, and making it fast are among your main concerns until that great milestone, the day she's outgrown it. Then you have to figure out what to do with it.

Crib renovation A crib can be turned into a child-sized sofa/spare bed. Remove one side, cover the mattress with a special fabric and add throw pillows.

Crib cradle If you can't get your baby to sleep, put springs or spring casters on the crib legs. You can rock the baby in the crib.

Double time In the middle of the night you want to change baby's soiled linens as quickly as possible, so both of you can go back to sleep. The job is done in half the time if you make up the bed with two sets of linens, separated by a waterproof sheet. In other words, there'll be six layers atop the mattress instead of three—top sheet, mattress pad, waterproof sheet, then a new top sheet, mattress pad, and waterproof sheet. Just strip off one set if a change is called for.

Clean and easy Don't discard your receiving blankets. Infants gurgle, drool, and spit up while lying abed, and it's a pain to have to change the whole sheet when one spot only is soiled. Tucking a receiving blanket into the ends of the crib where the child's head lies keeps the sheet clean and dry longer and saves time and wear and tear on sheets.

Changing Times

Bottoms up! There are arguments on both sides of the cloth diaper versus disposable issue and you will have to make the decision that's most comfortable for you. One thing parents will agree on is that having the changing table conveniently arranged, with a toy to distract baby, makes the process go as fast as possible. They will also advise you that it's fortunate that you become swift at diapering, because you will be called upon to do it frequently and in the most unlikely circumstances. While there is nothing discreet about a dirty diaper and it's not always possible to be discreet in the changing of it, there's no way to ignore a wailing wet or soiled baby. It's helpful if—along with a good supply of diapers, of course—you have a sense of humor. And when one day you admonish your child, "Just remember: I changed your diapers!" don't expect gratitude.

Balancing act If you're afraid the baby will fall off the changing table while you're using it, put a pad anywhere on the floor—or on your bed—and go to work.

Budget wipes Pull out the core of a roll of toilet paper, pour baby oil on one end of the roll, then pour more on the other end. Start pulling sheets from the inside, at the core. Store wipes in a covered container.

Diaper padding Get lap pads—rubber with a flannel surface—to protect any surface for diaper changes. Put them under the baby so you will not have to launder the sheeting on the changing pad. Put them over your shoulder when you're burping. And put them on the lap of the well-dressed visitor who wants to hold the baby.

Hair ways If the safety pin is too blunt to go through the diaper, run it through your hair. The bit of oil it will collect will help it to glide right through.

Paper hanger Put up a paper-towel holder near the changing table. Moistened paper towels are strong enough to clean a soiled baby bottom. The paper is handy for other spills, too.

Dry idea Cornstarch can promote yeast infections and inhaled talcum can be bad for lungs. See what your pediatrician recommends, and if you do use powder, don't shake it around. Sprinkle some into your hand, and then apply it—sparingly. Or pour it into a ten-inch square of clean cloth—an old T-shirt or a piece of old sheet will do. Gather and tie the ends and use as a powder puff. No waste.

Rash move We don't know who first discovered that liquid Mylanta—applied externally—is effective for diaper rash (just pour some into the palm of your hand and smooth it over the affected area), but lots of parents have tried it successfully. Diaper rash is caused by uric acid, and Mylanta's antacid formula apparently works as well on uric acid as it does on the bubbly acids in your stomach. And Mylanta or its generic equivalent is much cheaper than many creams and lotions. A little goes a long way, too. Please check with your pediatrician.

Bottoms up When you reach for a store-bought diaper wipe, often you'll find that the top ones are dry. That's because while the container sat in the store the liquid all settled to the bottom. If at home you store the container upside down, the liquid will be redistributed and the damp ones will be at the top—ready for use.

Container reuses Save empty wipe containers to use as toy boxes, snack boxes, jewelry boxes—or to hold homemade wipes.

Do-it-yourself wipes These baby wipes cost pennies and are environmentally friendly. In a container from the commercial wipes—or any waterproof container—stack up tissues or paper towels. Saturate with baby oil and water, mixed half and half.

Diapers undone Why do some babies delight in pulling the tapes off disposable diapers? Only the baby knows for sure. What we do know is that covering the diaper tape with an eight-inch strip of masking tape helps keep it in place. Or put the diaper on backward so your baby can't try this trick.

Doubling's less troubling To keep a soaked diaper from awakening your baby, provide some extra absorbency. Pull off and discard the outer plastic coating from a second clean diaper, and insert the unused absorbent pad inside the first. There are also commercial "Diaper Doublers."

Pointing in the right direction When changing a little boy's diaper, make sure the penis is pointing down before you fasten the sides. You'll avoid tummy leaks during the night.

Shoe 'nuff As you try to change the diaper, the baby will reach for everything on the changing table. After her child tried to eat talcum powder, one mother came up with this great idea: Adjacent to the changing table, hang a multipocket shoe holder to hold everything for changing the baby. Hang it where your baby can't reach it from the changing table or from the floor.

Don't blow up—blow out When changing diapers on her restless child becomes too much to bear, one enterprising mother turns to bubble gum. As soon as it's time for a change, she bites down on a double wad of sugarless bubble gum, and by the time the old diaper is off, she's blown a perfectly formed bubble that holds her little one's attention.

Solid Foods and Sloppy Eaters

It's a big step forward when a baby starts eating solids, and you may be surprised to discover that your baby has very distinctive tastes. It may become frustrating if certain foods are rejected and rebuffed. You'll need some creative ways to work around this problem, but don't let it worry you too much; repeated studies show that when offered a well-balanced menu (and not junk food) children will eat foods that over the course of a few days eventually give them the nutrients they need. Not long after solids are introduced, a baby will start eating finger food, and later develop the skills to use table implements, though not fast enough to suit most parents. Watching and supervising this process requires the patience of a saint and in ideal circumstances a dining room that can be hosed clean. The food winds up on the floor, walls, high chair, even the ceiling—everywhere except in baby's mouth. Obsessive-compulsives should leave the child in someone else's hands during mealtime. Sloppy eating starts at about six months and, from what we calculate, lasts until the child goes off to college.

Sweet stuff One pediatrician has parents introduce applesauce as the first solid. Many babies are more enthusiastic about its taste than the taste of the traditional cereal meal.

Baby mouthfuls A small plastic syringe or medicine dropper may be more useful than a spoon in getting your very young child to swallow just the right amount.

Rag time A wet washrag will appeal to a teething baby after mealtime. He'll enjoy chewing on it and he'll be cleaning his face at the same time!

Tray service Baby-food jars are exactly the same diameter as soda-pop cans. To carry a large stock of baby food from the grocery store, use an empty cardboard soda case: it will carry twenty-four jars easily.

Warm-ups A baby just starting on solid foods eats a very small amount, so you can't heat the whole jarful. A microwave- and dishwasher-safe egg poacher, with lid, is perfect for small portions. Each section can heat a different kind of food, and the lid makes storage easy if you want to premeasure meals for a quick warm-up.

Safety marker Baby food in jars can be wonderful, except when baby eats just a bit of veggie, a bit of meat, and a bit of fruit. Half-eaten jars are put away, and when someone else presides over the next meal, who's to know what's fresh and what's stale? Solve this problem with a permanent marker, stored inside the refrigerator. Use it to write the date and time food was last used—"9/30. A.M."—on the top of the lid. Tightly capped jarred food can be kept refrigerated for two or three days only. Then it should be discarded.

Dinner for one When children begin eating table food, they don't eat much of it and there's usually lots of waste and mess. An efficient solution is to store and serve baby-size portions of adult food (leftovers are excellent for this purpose) in paper muffin cups. Wrap in plastic wrap and freeze, then reheat as needed. Microwave is best, of course. (As with all microwaved foods, stir well before serving to make sure the food isn't *too* hot.) Servings will also slide easily from the muffin cups into a saucepan. Baby-sitters will appreciate this tip, and you'll know your child is eating well.

Play spoon Before you begin giving your baby solid foods, give her a spoon to use as a toy during the day. Make sure she carries the spoon when you bring her to the table. Feed her, with a clean spoon, as usual. She'll want to handle the new spoon herself before long. When she reaches for it, make sure there's a little food on it to taste. She'll see it gets into her mouth.

Little grippers Once your child is sitting in the high chair—at about six months or so—always be sure to use the straps to hold her in place. A rubber sink mat under the baby's bottom or rubber bathtub decals on the seat makes it less slippery.

Stick to the spoon Getting cereal, bananas, and milk on the same spoon takes more coordination than most toddlers possess. Thicken the milk first by stirring in a dollop or two of plain or matching fruit yogurt until it's pasty enough to hold the ingredients together on a spoon. Tastes good and helps your child.

Finger sandwiches Baby-food sandwiches may sound yucky to adults, but your child may devour a layer of baby-food meat spread on an open-faced slice of bread as if it were caviar on toast. Next step: a closed sandwich.

Food too hot Part 1 When baby food is too hot, drop in an ice cube and stir it around just long enough to lower the temperature. Remove the cube. The food will retain its texture, consistency, and flavor.

Food too hot Part 2 Freeze low-sodium chicken broth in an ice-cube tray to make cubes meant just to cool hot soups and stews quickly. Stirring a cube into the steaming bowl of food cools it fast enough for a hungry toddler.

Don't be a drip Tie a terry-cloth wristband or pony-tail holder around a toddler's wrist when he's eating runny food such as Popsicles, ice-cream cones, frozen ice, or watermelon.

Drip catcher At least an ice pop on the stick can't plop on the floor like an ice-cream cone. But it does drip. To catch the drips, cut a slit in a small paper plate or a muffin cup and insert the stick.

Fill 'er up Your restless toddler—at around a year and a half or two—may find mealtime more exciting if the serving dish isn't an ordinary dinner plate but a plastic boat or truck. Most plastic toys are nontoxic and dishwasher safe.

Food to get your hands around At some point toddlers lose interest in eating any food they can't hold in their hands. So go with the flow. Convert as many foods as possible into finger foods. Graspables include skinny toast strips, carrots cut lengthwise, buds of cauliflower and broccoli, circles of squash, and cucumber wedges.

Walking bowls Ever notice that when a toddler sticks a spoon in a plastic bowl full of food the bowl invariably takes a walk across the surface of the high-chair tray or dinner table and then, often, a high dive to the floor. Keep it in place by affixing a round rubber suction cup to the under side of the bowl. Moisten the suction cup on both sides first, make sure one adheres to the bowl, and press the bowl to the dining surface. Then fill it with food.

Teething

You'll soon have a new possible cause for baby's crying: teething. Before the day comes when you finally spot something hard and sharp and welcome inside your baby's mouth—those little teeth—your baby will be complaining. In fact, teething is reputed to cause everything from fretfulness to diarrhea to occasional fever. Don't grind your own teeth over your baby's teething pains. Follow these tips, and try to remember that when all those teeth are finally in, the days of jarred baby food will be behind you.

Something to chew on Many moms like frozen bagels as teething rings. Or use a banana frozen at peak ripeness. Peel it, cut in half widthwise, wrap or bag it, and then freeze it until needed. Commercial teethers won't taste half as good, or contain nutrients. On the other hand, small chunks of food may break off and are potentially hazardous. Keep an eye on your teething infant.

Ragtime And don't forget one of the most popular playground tips—put a wet washcloth in the freezer and take it out when it's nicely frozen. It makes a great chewy. If you soak it in fruit juice before you freeze it, not only will the cold relive the pain but also baby will enjoy sucking the juice.

Strip ease Instead of using a whole washcloth, or constantly searching for the teething ring, you can have plenty of teething aids on hand—at no cost. Take a clean rag or washcloth and tear it into strips, tie each in a knot, wash, and freeze it. Wash after using, of course, then freeze again.

Creative teething trick Giving a sick child a plastic medicine dropper to teeth on, instead of a teething ring, serves a dual purpose. It can help overcome resistance to taking medicine from the dropper when the time comes.

Tickle their ivories When your baby gets cranky from teething, let him chew on a soft toothbrush with a dab of Orajel (the commercial product that "numbs" gum on teething babies).

Aww, chew! When her baby wouldn't stop teething on the grocery-cart handle, one mom bought a length of plastic shower-rod cover, cut it to fit, washed it in soap and water, and took it to market. It covers the handle and keeps mom and baby happy. After the shopping trip, it's brought home and washed so it's ready to reuse.

Ready (Diaper Bag), Get Set (Stroller), and Go!

All parents, but particularly first-time parents, should make a special point to get out and about. You won't feel quite as overwhelmed by your new responsibilities if you go on some of the outings you normally would enjoy. If the baby's along, never leave home without a portable stroller and, of course, a well-equipped diaper bag. The mommy and daddy network has lots of tips for what goes into it as well as some advice on how not to forget it when you're rushing out the door.

In the bag Basic supplies for the diaper bag include bottles, an extra nipple (in case one drops), diapers, wipes, an extra sweater, toy(s), a washcloth, juice, treats, and a pacifier or teething ring.

A change for mom When loading a diaper bag before an outing, take along a spare blouse or shirt for mom, in case of wet burps or fruit-juice spills.

Emergency numbers Keep a set of emergency phone numbers in your diaper bag. Accidents can happen anywhere.

Money saver Baby-wipe traveling cases are a good idea, but they're costly, and a zippable plastic bag or a travel soap dish will do the job just as effectively. It will keep the wipes moist and it takes up less room, too. You can use commercial wipes or substitute a damp washcloth or a few pieces of moistened paper towel.

Wrapping it up Keep some light plastic bags—used to wrap produce or newspaper on rainy days—with the diaper bag to dispose of the soiled diapers. Tie a knot to kill the smell.

Rain or shine A small folding umbrella is a handy, compact addition to the diaper bag. It keeps off rain, it keeps off snow, and it's also a sunshade for the baby when the rest of the family is at play on the tennis court or ball field.

Spoon to go An adult-sized travel toothbrush container makes a sanitary container for an infant feeding spoon when you're on the go.

Separate compartments In the diaper bag, you can use one or two cosmetic bags (the clear plastic type) for small things that tend to rattle around and get lost in a large bag.

Stain away A stain-remover stick takes up hardly any room in the diaper bag and it's ready to treat stains immediately. Save time poking through dirty laundry later looking for stains.

The car keys? In the diaper bag, of course Getting yourself and the baby dressed and out of the house can be a hassle. No wonder you leave the diaper bag, refrigerated medicine, or baby food behind! One way to make sure you won't is to put the car keys in the bag (or on the medicine). When you're visiting someone's house, use the same trick so you will leave nothing behind.

Baby caddy If your baby has fallen asleep in the crib or baby seat by the time you're ready to go out, try putting her down in the stroller. Then jump in the shower, get dressed, and head on out.

Back saver Why not stop back problems *before* they start? *Never* bend over to lift a child (or anything else) without sucking in your stomach first. Keep your back straight and bend your knees slightly at the same time, so the strain is distributed downward, not concentrated in the bundle of muscles (and nerves) in the small of your back.

String-along snack When is a bagel like a yo-yo? When it's tied with a short (but not too short) string to your baby's stroller bar, so it returns without hitting the ground when baby drops it—or throws it. Kids love chewing on something while they're rolling along. Bagels fit the bill—and are the only snack that's fit to be tied.

Clip service Attach a small toy to the stroller or diaper bag with a mitten clip. The child can reach it and it won't get lost.

Memories Are Made of This

It's astonishing how quickly your child passes through babyhood. When you have a five-year-old, you can barely remember rocking your newborn daughter to sleep or recall how your little one-year-old boy spent his days. Memories that you can preserve will be cherished not only by you but by your child. Children have enormous curiosity about what they were like when they were little. (And, by the way, they will want to remember what their parents and grandparents were like in those days, too, so remember to take films and photos of everyone, not just baby.) While it's easy today to capture baby's first steps, first words, and first haircut on film, videotape, or on a cassette sound recorder, don't forget there are other traditional and personal means of preserving and recording your child's progress.

Grand (parents') gift An ideal gift for grandparents who live far away is a large three-ring photo binder. Keep a supply of empty plastic pages in your house, fill them with photos of you and the kids, and periodically send them off to grandpa and grandma. All they have to do is insert the pages and they'll have an ongoing, constantly updated record of the grandchildren that they can show off. And they won't have stray photos all over the house.

Oral history Instead of always buying prerecorded tape, have grandparents record their favorite stories—nursery tales or real stories. Passing these tapes along to future generations is a great way to start a new tradition.

The big board A wall calendar with large date blocks is a smart means of keeping track of all the memorable things that happen during your baby's first years. You can mark down special dates quickly and record those special moments and first words without having to run for the baby book.

Too cute to throw out Don't throw away, give away, or store those especially cute little baby outfits—dresses, suits, socks—that make babies look so adorable you almost wish they'll never grow up. Turn them into "stuffed dolls" or even frame the ones you always thought should be in a museum. The "adorable outfit" phase doesn't last long, as every parent knows.

Doll clothes Even if you're not planning another child, save infant clothing and diapers for any "little mother" in the house. She will like them for her baby dolls.

Dear diary Keeping a child's journal is a wonderful remembrance for parent and child and has an immediate effect as well. Composing your thoughts daily (or every other day) is a discipline with its own reward. Approach it as if you were writing a letter to the child, and don't worry about length or subject. Recording just a few sentences about the child's behavior, noting down an anecdote, or jotting down a bright moment will invoke memories in the future. Don't forget to include your own feelings about being a parent. A bound book with blank pages is ideal for this purpose.

Family tree How many cousins do I have? Where does Aunt Liz live? How many brothers does daddy have? How is Pop-Pop related to me? It's wonderful to compile a family tree that will help answer these questions that children love to ask. When your child gets older, he or she can help you add to the tree and illustrate each "limb" with photos. The page can be photocopied and sent to relatives at Christmastime.

Making their mark You can record your child's growth on the back of the closet door or wall. Or hang a yardstick, and make the marks and record the date on that. (It's a way to save the information if you repaint.) Children love looking back and seeing how much they've grown.

Babyproofing

If your baby is healthy and curious about the world around her, she may poke fingers, nose, and feet into places no one has ever thought of going before, and what she can't put herself into, she may try to put into herself. There are a lot of reasons to babyproof—not just to protect the child from the world around her, but also to protect the world around her from the child.

Since the world isn't babyproofed A youngster's natural curiosity will impel him to want to touch everything he sees, but since much of the world is not babyproofed, this is potentially dangerous. Train your child to back off when you say "No!"—and if you have to say it loud enough to startle the child (and maybe even provoke a startled cry), that's okay. Otherwise you may not make your point. Once the child has been trained, he's prepared to visit homes where there is no babyproofing. You want your child to learn to be a welcome guest in a world of books and coffee tables so mommy (and everyone else in the room) can relax.

Hands off Rather than saying "no" constantly, you might prefer this tactic (if you have the patience and a child on whom it works). Persuade your child to wave to the pretty object that attracts her attention. You wave, too. Surprisingly enough, this alternative may be diverting enough to satisfy the child's curiosity without damping her enthusiasm.

Hands-on possibilities After childproofing, replace some of your breakables (vases, picture frames, etc.) with Tupperware bowls filled with small toys or blocks. This keeps "No" and "Don't touch" commands to a minimum and allows the child to satisfy his curiosity when exploring his home environment.

Over the top The absolutely easiest way to keep an open door from closing on baby's fingers is to throw a towel over the top. This is especially useful if there's another child coming in and out of the room. (But if there's a heating unit overhead, make sure the towel isn't a fire hazard.)

Liberty bells When toddlers roam, it's hard keeping track of them—unless they have little Christmasy sleighbells tied to their shoelaces. The reassuring patter of the bells will remind you that your baby's roaming safely. Bells should be attached not to the ends of the laces but near one of the eyes of the shoes. Otherwise, the bells could wind up in the baby's mouth.

Shadow cabinet If you spend a lot of time in your kitchen, and it's completely babyproofed, how is your baby to stay amused while you keep an eye on her? Set aside one floor-level cabinet that the baby is allowed to go into. Stock it with unbreakable kitchen utensils, some of baby's own toys, or a mix of both. This way you won't have to carry toys from playroom to kitchen and back again.

Dutch treat If the baby can play in the room adjacent to the kitchen, install a Dutch door or screen door. The baby can see mom and dad—and they can see her. While a gate serves the same purpose, an older child may be tempted to crawl over it.

Stepping up in the world Instead of putting a safety gate at the bottom of the stairs, put it on the stairs, several steps up. This method gives little climbers a sense of daring and accomplishment. But make sure the stairs or the floor is carpeted to absorb inevitable tumbles.

Bubble wrapping Sharp corners on coffee tables can be childproofed with a piece of plastic bubble wrap. Cut the bubble wrap into triangles and secure them with masking tape.

Padded cushions Shoulder pads make perfect corner cushions for sharp-edged dining-room tables. Tape them to the bottom of the table so the tape won't mar the finish, fold them up so they fit the corners, and put your tablecloth on top. Or sew the pads to two elastic strips that will stretch diagonally across the table.

Saving soles Shiny waxed floors and kids in socks are not compatible. Older children ought to know better than to run in socks, but toddlers don't. Nonskid socks for little ones can be fashioned by applying dabs of "puff paints" on the soles of their socks. For better adherence of paint to fabric, stretch the socks over baby's shoes before applying. No shoes yet? Use a small juice glass as a "shoe form."

Rough and ready The first thing to do with baby's first pair of real shoes is to sandpaper the soles. Scratch them up thoroughly so baby won't slip taking his first step. Works on leather or vinyl.

A Christmas story Halfway through the happy task of decorating the new baby's first Christmas tree and tying it to the wall to prevent it from toppling over, a smart dad wondered about the chances of his baby's pulling an ornament off the tree and eating the shards when it broke. After a brief ponder, mom and dad decided to leave the lower branches barren of decoration—but that left the tree looking half-dressed. Now mom had an idea. "Let's gather some of baby's toys, especially the ones with handles, and fix them on the lower branches." And so they did. Their baby must have felt she'd made a contribution because after removing just one small rattle she never touched "her" decorations again. (One small holiday miracle.)

A different view After you think you're finished babyproofing your house, both parents should get down on their hands and knees for a final inspection from baby's perspective. You'll look silly crawling on all fours, but you'll see things an adventurous toddler wouldn't miss.

Bend a little Some kids—and cats—can't keep their paws off the toilet-paper roll. It's a wasteful and annoying habit. But if you squeeze the entire roll tightly before inserting it on the holder, enough to bend the cardboard inside, tiny hands or paws can't set it spinning.

Book protection Much-loved books for toddlers are much-handled both by you and by them. Obviously, you want to encourage a loving relationship with books, but you don't want the books to be "loved to death." To increase the life span of classics such as *Goodnight Moon* or *Where's Spot?* cover each page with clear Contact paper. Then you don't have to worry about tears and/or scribbles.

All secure Make sure that those tall book and toy shelves are securely fastened to the wall. Otherwise, baby may tip them over.

Door stopper Put a happy face or other decal on a glass door at eye level so your child will see it, and accidents will be prevented.

First aid Your pediatrician may have some recommendations for your home first-aid kit. Don't forget the syrup of ipecac, to induce vomiting in case a child has swallowed poison; but never administer this without calling the poison control center first. (Check the expiration date: the product doesn't last forever.)

Getting around the corners Slice tennis balls open and use them as cushions for sharp corners on furniture. Just use a knife to slit them halfway open, then use one entire ball on each corner.

Knee protection Crawling along wooden country floors or boardwalks or decks is okay if they're enclosed so that a baby can't tumble down steps or through the railing. But what about the possibility of scraped knees? Cutting the elastic tops off your old sweatsocks and fitting them around your baby's knees will nip the problem in the bud.

Shock treatment Don't forget to cover *outdoor* electrical sockets when you're childproofing your home. Covers will keep out crawling infants and toddlers, and moisture, as well.

Fit to be tied When her nine-month-old persisted in standing up or attempting to climb out of the shopping cart during every market visit, one mother's concern for safety took precedence over orthodoxy. As soon as her child was seated, she tied his shoelaces together, making it impossible for him to get his feet through the holes to stand up. Trying kept him busy—and safe—while mom concentrated on her work. As he got older, he stopped trying to get out.

Tub Time

First-time parents are often terrified of tub time, because bathing a baby is frightening if you've never done it. Once you've become accustomed to the routine, it's very possible your baby may have become terrified of the bath. Fortunately this is a transient phase. Most children quickly learn to enjoy the tub and will play happily in it for hours—though of course, you should never leave a young child unattended in the water. The only part little ones don't like is having their hair washed, but some parents have suggestions for making this task less tear provoking.

Slip sliding away The sink makes the most convenient place to wash a young baby; it's a far more convenient height than the tub.

Warm-ups If your baby is protesting his bath, make sure the room is comfortably warm. Putting a towel at the bottom of the sink or tub makes the bath safer and also more comfortable, since baby's body doesn't touch the cold porcelain.

Water babies Being plunked into the middle of a big tub can be frightening for an infant too little to hold on to the sides. Instead, put the baby into a plastic laundry basket that's been placed in the middle of the tub.

Temperature control Floating the bottle of baby lotion or shampoo in the water makes it warmer and less of a shock when applied to your child's skin or hair.

Ducky idea Keep bath toys in a plastic beach bucket, and poke holes in the bottom so the water can drain away.

Recycling plastic Don't throw away plastic pump bottles from liquid hand soaps. Refilling the pump bottles with baby shampoo helps cut down on waste, and gives you a freer hand during shampoo time.

Rub-a-dub-dub, two in the shower Sometimes daddy feels shortchanged. If he's going off to work, he's too rushed in the morning to spend time with the baby and it's bedtime shortly after he gets home. One way for him to spend time with an older infant is to hold him in the shower. (Dad may be more comfortable draping a towel over his arm and cradling the baby in that. To be on the safe side, mom should be there to hand over the baby at the beginning of the shower and receive the baby once it is finished.

Set for safety The hot-water temperature in many houses is higher than necessary. If you turn it down to below 125 degrees F.

(or have the plumber do so), there won't be any chance of scalding. Also make it a habit—and teach the child to make it a habit—to turn the cold-water tap on first when you're running bathwater, whether anyone's in the tub or not. Even if the hot water at home is regulated to run warm rather than hot, this habit may prevent accidental scalding when staying at a hotel or visiting another home. The same rule should apply to the shower: cold water on first, off last.

Drain storm Some little ones fear being sucked down the drain when the tub empties of water. Leave the water in the tub until your child is out of the bath, and maybe even until the child has left the bathroom.

Hair raising Children sometimes kick up a fuss when it's time to have their hair washed. Make it something they look forward to by allowing them to wash their hair (and each other's) with a squirt gun.

Bubbling personality Bubble baths are great for luring reluctant (or stubborn) little ones into the tub. But hard-core cases need extra perks, like spare bubble wands they can use to blow their own bubbles while you scrub them clean.

Sock of soap Two-year-olds may think they know how to wash themselves but few can manage a bar of soap without getting it in their eyes or having it go ballistic. Slip a small sock over a bar of soap, knot it closed, and put an end to unguided missiles in the tub. Your child will have a personal washcloth/soap holder that won't slip away.

Bath's over Getting children to leave the tub is the other side of getting them into the tub in the first place. Kids love any sort of game, so when they won't leave, challenge them to a race.

The winner(s) have to be out and dry—and must have collected tub toys in the proper container—by the time the water drains. You can award stars on a chart for incentive.

Pictures on the ceiling Some kids have a mortal fear of getting shampoo in their eyes no matter how convincing the manufacturer's claim that his product is formulated to produce "no tears." The minute you attempt to tilt their heads back for the rinse, they start thrashing around dangerously. Fortunately, as all parents quickly learn, children are easily distracted, even at moments of stress. Mount a favorite poster or picture, perhaps a cartoon character or a scene from a fairy tale, on the ceiling directly over the tub. While you cradle your child's head securely with one hand, encourage him to look straight up at the poster or picture while you use a shower hose or cup with the other hand to give him a proper rinse. Or paste stars on the ceiling and ask the child to count them during the rinse.

Mirror, mirror Here's a perfectly silly game guaranteed to keep a child still while you're working on her hair. Tell the child to concentrate on keeping her mirror image from moving. The one who moves first loses. When your child moves (it's inevitable), tell her you'll give the mirror image another chance and play the game again.

Net benefits Keeping bathroom toys in a string bag keeps them together and allows them to dry off. The bag can be hung from the shower head to drain. When it comes time for beach or pool play, the child's water toys are in one place. Just grab the bag and go.

Kitchen aids Little ones often don't care where their "toys" come from, so long as they're fun and fascinating. Kitchen utensils—funnels, strainers, a slotted spoon—make wonderful playthings for the bath. You'll never run out of them, and when the baby's bored with one, it goes back to full-time kitchen duty.

Hair apparent Giving a child a haircut in the tub makes a lot of sense. Just put a net over the drain to trap loose hair. And have her wear a swim mask so you won't hear complaints about hair in the eyes. Littlest ones can be plunked into a high chair in the tub.

Neat and trim After the bath you may want to give your toddler's hair a trim. After combing bangs, press a long strip of clear tape on the hair above and below where you intend to cut. It will give you a straighter edge and the job will take half the time. There's hardly any cleanup because the shorn hair will stick to the tape.

The Smartly Dressed Child

It's fun to dress a baby like a doll, but while a doll just lies there while you dress it up, a baby is usually not nearly so cooperative. Plus—again unlike a doll—a young child spits up, drools, and spills things. It's nice to dress your child like a fashion plate for a special photograph, but for everyday, moms agree, go for what's practical and not for what's precious.

Fashion victims Some designers of baby clothes seem never to have dressed a small child. Baby clothes that you should avoid include garments that must be completely removed so a baby can be changed; that have tiny buttons or other difficult fasteners; or that include shirts that must be tucked in. (Overalls are a better design for a little one.) And don't buy anything newborn size for a full-term baby. It will be outgrown instantly.

Fashion victors When baby-shower time approaches, tell your friends that if they're intending to buy baby clothes you prefer one-piece outfits. No matter how fashionable they look in the store, two-piece outfits always ride up or fall down, while one-piece outfits stay neat and comfortable and can always be layered with pants or an extra sweater, depending on the weather.

The one-piece exception The only one-piece outfit for a baby that may not be practical is the one-piece snowsuit. While these have the advantage that they don't ride up and expose the baby's tummy, they require quite a bit of pushing and pulling to get the baby inside. If you're in and out of stores—and your child is being exposed to sudden temperature changes—you may prefer to use a sacklike garment to cover the baby's legs and a jacket on the top. It's much easier to slip a baby in and out of the sack and zip and unzip a jacket than to take a snowsuit off and put it on again.

Getting socked Sorting socks is time consuming and, as everyone knows, the washing machine is to single socks what the Bermuda Triangle is to boats. Here are three alternatives to solve the problem of matches:

- Use a mesh lingerie-washing bag for your baby's socks.
- Use a safety pin to keep the socks together before you do the laundry. The best place to keep the pins is alongside the hamper, along with a stain-remover stick.
- Buy all white socks, all in the same design. No sorting necessary.

Safety and numbers Buy multiples of such things as pajamas, mittens, and socks so you won't always be looking for the match. With the mittens, do it at the beginning of the season so you won't have trouble finding duplicates.

Giveaway boxes Pack outgrown clothes in old diaper boxes, and label the boxes by season and size. Its much easier to locate appropriate giveaways.

Patchwork To make clothes last longer, sew or iron on patches inside the knees. (If you make patches, cut them with pinking shears. That makes a zigzag edge that won't unravel.) (Children like fun patches that you can make by tracing cookie cutter shapes onto fabric.) Long pants can turn into shorts, and stretchies can be expanded, if you cut off bottoms and sew on socks or terry booties with rubber bottoms.

Playing footsies If your child wears socks inside the all-in-one sleeper, the pajamas will stay in place better. When the plastic feet are outgrown, ripped, or too slippery, just cut them off. To keep tootsies warm at night, your child can wear socks.

Sizing up Your baby will probably increase in size significantly during the first year but don't start buying very large clothes on the assumption this growth rate will continue. Eventually, the child will pass through every size, but if you've bought size 5 winter clothes and she's size 5 in the spring, that's no help. The only things to buy ahead are nonseasonal items like socks, hats, underwear, or loose, baggy sweaters and jackets.

Slipons One surefire way to get boots on over shoes or sneakers is to put a plastic bag over each shoe. Then the shoe slides smoothly into the boot.

Fit to be tied Sneaker laces will stay tied if you dampen them first. Using elastic instead of laces makes slipping shoes on and off easier since you needn't untie them, and elastic is less likely to come untied.

Stretch and go Sew buttons on with elastic thread or fishing line. Elastic makes it less likely the buttons will pop off, and fishing line is sturdiest.

Perfectly suitable Last year's sweatsuits can become this year's pajamas and next year's cutoffs.

No clowning around Toddlers may look cute flopping around in all-in-one pajamas if the feet are too big—like a circus clown's—but it's no joke when they trip and fall down. To prevent this, put terry-cloth-and-elastic wrist bands (like the ones tennis players wear) or the terry-and-elastic knee protectors, worn by crawling infants, around the toddler's ankles. Pull the feet of the all-in-one up through the elastic until they fit your child's feet comfortably.

Sam, you made the pants too long Pants are quickly outgrown, so there's no point in making a hem if they are too long. (Besides, it's extra work and leaves a mark along the cuff.) To keep them from dragging on the ground and tripping your toddler, slide inexpensive tennis players' wrist bands around her ankles or put some elastic around the bottom (inside the cuff) so you can push them up.

Unisex rompers If you're planning on having more than one child, make an effort to buy unisex rompers, jumpsuits, pajamas, and snowsuits in neutral colors so they can be handed down to younger siblings.

Time-saver Keep a stick-type laundry stain remover on the changing table or tie one on a string attached to your hamper. Treat stained clothes as soon as they come off the child's body and toss them in the hamper. You won't have to go through every item in the hamper when you do gather the laundry.

Buying Time

The first time your child climbs out of the crib and comes toddling into your room, you're thrilled at the accomplishment. Then you realize that his independence means you will no longer be able to safely snatch a few extra moments of sleep in the morning. Young toddlers, who are independent and fearless, and also fiercely demanding of your attention, can be particularly time consuming, but looking after young children of any age doesn't give you many moments for yourself, let alone your other duties. It is difficult to find time to do your kitchen chores, make a phone call, take a bath—anything, in fact, but play with the child. But here are some suggestions from the playground to buy yourself a few minutes here and there.

The sound of music No little one needs an alarm clock to wake her up. However, a clock alarm can keep her amused. If your child wakes, as most do, at a particular time each morning, preset a clock radio for that time, tuned to a music station that she might enjoy. She may delay calling you long enough to allow you a few minutes' extra sleep.

Baby toys If you're absolutely desperate for something to amuse a small baby, keep in mind that the "something" doesn't have to be a toy. Babies can play for minutes at a time with Scotch tape (or bandages) and ice cubes. Also toilet-paper rolls, plastic containers, and cards.

Toy time A special "early-morning" toy basket—with items that have novelty value—may occupy your child while you get some extra sleep. Change the toys or add to the stock occasionally to keep the child interested. (Put aside some toys just for this purpose; recycled items are interesting anew.)

Creamy stuff No one's home except you and the toddler and you have to take a shower and get your makeup on—quickly. Luckily, your shower has sliding glass doors, so you grab some shaving cream and Psss-hh! plant a blob of it on the outside. Baby can't wait to put his hands in it, and by the time he's finished his finger painting, you're ready to go. Or do this on a tile wall.

Cooking up some fun Entertaining a toddler and cooking dinner at the same time are easy if you spread a large absorbent beach towel under the high chair first, then provide your little chef with some lukewarm water in a shallow pan, a small sieve, funnel, measuring cup, and spoon. She'll love the freedom of figuring out new recipes and your cleanup is easy.

Telephone toys Parents who must mind small children while working at home know how hard it is to conduct a business conversation while a toddler competes for your attention. A "mystery box" with a "surprise" toy inside—strategically placed near your home-office phone—can be a lifesaver when an important client calls. Rotate the surprise inside occasionally so the child doesn't get bored. An answering machine that can be adjusted to pick up either on two or four rings is another home-office essential, for times when you're at the changing table or just need an extra second or two to make sure your baby is safe and secure before you dash to the phone. An answering machine with a built-in portable cellular phone is handy as well.

Learning to play Putting a baby in a crib with some toys may not work if the baby hasn't learned how to amuse himself. A good time to encourage the baby to start playing alone in the crib is when he's relaxed and contented, after a bath or a meal. Doing this on a regular basis works best and lets both of you enjoy a free moment.

Morning games Parents who wish to catch an extra hour's sleep on Sunday mornings rather than being awakened by an early-rising toddler may place a few of her favorite (and safest) toys in a plastic bucket and (after she's fallen asleep) tie it securely inside but at the foot of the crib. Most likely, the child's natural curiosity will draw her to the bucket and, with any luck, she'll busy herself for an hour while you snooze.

Shaping up If you must take your child jogging, you need an expensive jogging stroller. A cheaper alternative (and as effective a way to exercise) is to take your child for a ride on your stationary bike. Don't cradle the child in your arms. Put him in a Snugli, strapped securely to your chest. The monotony of the spinning wheel may cause him to drift off to sleep. When the child gets older, you can attach an infant seat to your outdoor bike and take your little one for a ride—provided he's wearing a helmet, of course.

Juiced up For an early riser, leave a "pop-up" thermos (with its built-in straw) in the fridge, filled with a favorite morning drink. There won't be any breaks or spills, and you can have a few extra minutes of sleep.

In their cups How many times a day do you have to fill juice cups for little ones? Cut down. After breakfast, tell your children to put their favorite cups in the refrigerator rather than in the sink or dishwasher. Fill the cups immediately. They will be there, full, when it's juice time again. Tell children always to return the empty cups to the fridge. Whenever your work brings you near the fridge, replenish the cups.

Two for one The best way to have more time for yourself when your child is about a year old is to develop a friendship with the mother of a child you know your little one gets along with. See it as the start of a long-term friendship, and know it makes exchange baby-sitting easier. However, if you discover you have very different parenting styles, you may have to find another buddy for this purpose.

Duty shifts Why should both parents have to get up with the kids on the weekend? If you designate one weekend morning for each parent to sleep late, your child or children will get some one-on-one time while the other parent has some time to read, catch up on correspondence, talk on the phone—or sleep.

The morning line Part 1 When a child reaches the age of three or thereabouts, and you'd like to catch an extra hour's sleep in the morning, tell her she's old enough to help herself to a pre-breakfast snack you've set up the night before, and there's no need to wake mommy and daddy first thing in the morning. Place the snack on a low counter in the kitchen. Dry cereal, cheese, crackers, and juice in a plastic cup with a lid should suffice. Make sure the snack is food your child isn't likely to choke on. Preset the television to a children's channel, and show her how to turn on the set.

Morning line Part 2 A variation on the above (suitable for the slightly older child) is to let your child choose his own breakfast cereal the night before. Set the table with the cereal-filled bowl covered with plastic wrap and pour just the right amount of milk into a plastic measuring cup on a low shelf in the refrigerator alongside juice in paper cups. And leave a roll of paper towels handy.

Junior baby-sitters Children in the neighborhood aged eight to eleven may not be old enough to baby-sit on their own, but if they enjoy playing with your children, hire them to come over after school occasionally or on a regular basis. They can play with the children while you are freed up to work on a project that requires your concentration—a nice sanity break!—yet you are there in the event your presence is required.

Reading fee Telling a particularly motivated older child that the best thing she could do for her siblings is to teach them something might be enough of an incentive. Sweetening the deal with a cash reward may even lure a reluctant older sibling to take up the offer. The point of the deal is to inspire the older child to read to a younger one. Make it easy for all concerned by picking the book, setting up a cozy corner filled with pillows and a bowl of munchies, and if necessary offering a few pointers. Pay by the quarter hour or by the number of pages. It's a great way to get the kids together and get them involved in reading.

Caretakers and Sitters: When You Go Out

Hiring a full-time sitter is a bigger undertaking than hiring someone who'll be watching your child for only an afternoon or evening, but of course your concern is the same: Will the person you leave in charge be kind and reliable? Will your child be comfortable and safe? Parents can't stress enough the importance of excellent word-of-mouth recommendations before you hire and sensitivity to your child's behavior afterward to gauge whether things are going as they should. As the employer, you can also make it easier on your sitter or nanny by being as clear as possible about your wishes and letting your child know that the baby-sitter is in charge when you aren't there. Sometimes the baby-sitting problem is simply the lack of a baby-sitter—and the parents on the playground have some remedies for that, too.

Briefings and debriefings Once you've hired a full-charge caretaker, plan to spend a week or two with her and the child before leaving her alone as the sole caregiver. Afterward, listen carefully to anything your child has to say about her. Does the child have any complaints? Are there any changes in your child's behavior that may indicate the sitter isn't up to the responsibilities of her job or is temperamentally unsuited to it? Is the child excessively happy or plainly relieved to see you when you come home? Is the child always sleeping when you come home or unusually cranky prior to the sitter's arrival? These may be signs that indicate the sitter and child are not getting along.

Medical authorizations In the event of a medical emergency, it is helpful for parents to leave a notarized form authorizing the regular baby-sitter to permit emergency treatments in your absence. Put it in an envelope with copies of insurance forms and your list of numbers to call in an emergency, and put the envelope in the diaper bag so the sitter will have it at home and on outings. Make copies for a relative or anyone with whom you will be leaving your child if you are going out of town.

Number game Leave a baby-sitter with a detailed sheet of information, including the address and phone number where you will be, your time of return, the name of your doctor, and the name of a neighbor to call in an emergency. Everyone should know (but remind the sitter, anyway) that in case of emergency, it's faster and more efficient to dial 911 than to call the fire company or police or an ambulance service directly. If you have a pet, leave the name of your vet. Finally, be sure to put your home phone number and address on the sheet. When calling for help in an emergency a flustered sitter may not remember these critical pieces of information.

Mealtime stress reliever Many times a child's own parents have a hard time getting her to eat. When a baby-sitter has to prepare or supervise the children's meal, make things easier all around by planning a menu that you know your child won't balk at. Sometimes a child who dislikes having a sitter may even be persuaded to look forward to the occasion if a favorite meal will be served.

A reminder that mommy cares If you want to give a present to a child as a bribe when you go out, let the child—and sitter—know that it won't be handed over until the parents have left the house. It isn't necessary to buy something extravagant. A small trinket or edible will do, but make sure it's special. Perhaps it may even be gift-wrapped with loving care. Or leave behind a "secret surprise" hidden in an easily found spot. Cries of "Don't go! Please don't go!" vanish in the excitement of this activity. Don't be surprised—or offended—when the next day your child encourages you to go out again.

Coop baby-sitting Difficulty in getting baby-sitters for unexpected nights on the town is a frequent complaint among parents. And the added cost of a baby-sitter makes it easier to put off a sorely needed "date" with the spouse you hardly see anymore because your schedules are so full. One solution is to form a baby-sitting coop among the parents of your children's playmates. Here are some ground rules to get you started:

- The coop should issue a predetermined number of coupons to each member. Each coupon is worth a half-hour's time. Initial distribution may be worth a total of two hours.
- Members should agree beforehand on hours of availability.
- Coupons are surrendered to the baby-sitting parents, thus adding to their time bank.
- It's a good idea for the members to get together once a

month to see who's holding the most coupons and who the least.

- The coop also provides an opportunity for all the parents to have a social gathering (with kids, of course).

Job market If your regular baby-sitter is busy and you have no one else to call, offer the baby-sitter a small "finder's fee" if she can provide a substitute. Reassure her that when you need a sitter in the future you'll always call her first, and not her substitute.

Tearful goodbyes Most children are intuitively good at making you feel guilty when you leave them behind, and you may be treated to a tearstorm when you're ready to leave for an evening out. If you are confident that the child is in good hands, go ahead with your plans. The longer you prolong the goodbyes, the worse it gets. Almost inevitably, the minute you leave your child will return to his usual good spirits. It helps, of course, if you leave behind a special video or other diversion to help the baby-sitter out.

Tape companion As a baby-sitter's helper, one mother taped herself telling her child a bedtime story and singing a lullaby. This "personal treatment" worked like a charm to calm the child at bedtime.

Day Care and Separation

It's one thing to stay home and watch mommy or daddy leave; it's quite another for your baby to leave the house and go off to the day-care center herself. There are cases to be made for day care provided by a single adult in a home-type situation or for sending a youngster to a school-like environment, but you may not have a great many options. Still, you'll always want to check out the day care as carefully as possible, and you will need to find ways to comfort your young child as she separates not only from you but from the familiar home environment.

Checking it out Watching the early-morning arrivals at the day-care center you're considering should give you a clue as to whether it's the right place for you. Do the children seem eager to go in? Do the parents seem to be people you'd find compatible?

- An unexpected daytime visit gives you a different perspective from a formal visit, when the center is putting its best foot forward.
- Also check: Is the center licensed? What are staff qualifications? What's the staff/child ratio? Are unannounced visits allowed and/or encouraged? Are the children divided up by age? Is there a structured or "open" classroom? Is there a doctor on staff or as a consultant? Are facilities used away from the primary site? Are children mostly from the immediate neighborhood? Are facilities adequate and safe? Is the center close to your home or office? Are the disciplining procedures compatible with yours? Does the day-care center accept children who aren't toilet-trained?

Name branding If your child is in day care it is helpful to label everything—from the bottle to the clothing. One of the fastest ways to do this is with a rubber stamp, easily purchased from your local office-supply store (and also available through mail-order catalogs). You can stamp the child's name onto pressure-sensitive labels, and affix them to books, toys, etc. If you buy a permanent ink pad, you can even use rubber stamps to mark inside clothing, boots, etc.

Family keepsake A family picture taped to the inside of your child's cubby may help reassure her that her family is thinking of her when she's in nursery school or day care. Or send along a little photo album. It's amazing how comforting it can be for a child to look at a picture of mommy and daddy when the homesick blues strike.

Soothing sounds A tape of the child's favorite lullabies may be offered to the school. This can be played on the child's own cassette player or it may be enjoyed by all the children at nap time.

Accentuate the positive When your little one gives you that doleful look when you're saying goodbye at the day-care center or nursery school, don't ever say you "have to go," or that you're "late for work." All your child cares about is when you're coming back, so be reassuring. "I'll be back as soon as you're finished, you don't have to worry" is all you have to say. Let your child know where you're going, too. A drive past the place you work, if possible, may reassure your child that mommy or daddy is safe while he's at play.

Holdups If your child is concerned about separating, hand over a small item of yours and ask that he hold it for you until the end of the day. The idea that you will be returning is very comforting and may make parting a sweeter sorrow.

A funny thing happened on the way to school An imaginative mom solved the problem of separating from her child at day school by always having a very brief anecdote to tell the teacher about what happened on the way to school that day, making a point of telling it in front of the child. It can be anything—the color of the sky, a dog crossing the street, the first daffodil, or a cute little bird—as long as it appeals to a child's imagination and provides a distracting thought.

School anxiety If your nursery school or kindergarten child can't stand parting from you every morning, maybe mommy ought to alternate this duty. If one parent takes the morning shift, your child has the other to look forward to at day's end. From the child's point of view, that's just great.

Boo-boos and Other Medical Bugaboos

Taking that first step brings your baby one step closer to that first fall, and no one reacts—make that overreacts—like a toddler. Minor cuts and bruises can seem like war wounds to a small child, especially when there's blood and plenty of it. Scalp wounds, for instance, bleed a lot, and even a rough, tough ten-year-old boy will blanch at the sight of his own blood. Stopping the flow of blood from a wound is, of course, always the prime consideration. But getting rid of the sight of the blood and alleviating the pain are important steps in calming the child's fears. Other minor medical procedures also require your patience and imagination, as does calming fears of doctor visits. But what's a parent for if not to kiss away a hurt and comfort a fearful child?

Boo-boo bears A washcloth sewn into the shape of a bear makes a handy ice bag that not only soothes the pain of minor scrapes and bruises, but also serves to take tiny minds off the hurt.

Camouflage cloth Keep a couple of bright red washcloths handy for wiping away blood from cuts and scrapes. The sight of a bloodstain on a light-colored cloth can provoke hysteria over even the most minor casualty. Not only does the red hide the blood, but you may even be able to distract and calm a child by letting him watch the blood "disappear" as the antiseptic and a bandage are being applied.

It won't hurt! Removing Band-Aids or any adhesive bandage from a child's skin without any pain is easy if you gently rub a layer of petroleum jelly around the parts of the bandage sticking to the skin. Wait about sixty seconds. The jelly will dissolve the adhesive and the bandage can be lifted painlessly.

Disappearing act Hydrogen peroxide is great for getting blood out of clothes, sheets, and pillowcases. Or try salt water. Both of these remedies should be used when the stain is fresh. Removing a set-in bloodstain is almost impossible.

Night games A child who reacts violently to having cream applied or her fingernails clipped won't utter a peep if you wait until the middle of the night when she is in deep sleep.

Heat rash During the summer, your child is likely to suffer from heat rash. Dab on milk of magnesia generously. It dries white, can be easily washed off, and works well. Use as needed. (But don't mistake another type of rash for heat rash. Check with your pediatrician if you aren't absolutely certain of the cause.)

Home remedy Here's a medically safe hint for children prone to mild rashes after eating hard-to-resist but highly acidic foods (tomatoes, strawberries, etc.). Maalox antacid liquid, when applied directly to a rash, alleviates pain and redness at once.

Ice sculpture Plastic, water-filled, no-melt sculpted "ice cubes" are great distractions and pain relievers for minor bumps and bruises. Keep them in a freezer bag, let your child decide whether a heart, a fish or a bear will ease the pain faster, and dispense as necessary.

A stitch in time Jot down the name of a competent plastic surgeon, preferably one who has some experience with kids and cosmetic surgery and is recommended by your pediatrician, in case stitches are ever needed. It can make the difference between a scar carried for life and one that isn't. If there is a place you visit routinely (a weekend house, grandma's home), it's helpful to have a local recommendation for there as well.

One from Column A Take those packages of mustard or duck sauce served with Chinese food and keep them in the freezer. They're fine for putting tiny cold packs on bruises, and a frozen duck-sauce packet is more fun to use than an ice pack.

Fat lip? When a child falls and injures her lip or gums and the bruise requires ice, give her a frozen pop to suck on. She'll get the benefit of a "cold pack" that she can hold easily and enjoy in the process. A banana pop is best because it has no acid that will hurt a wound. Or keep a liquid-filled teething ring in your freezer, and whenever you have to take care of a swollen or bloody lip or mouth, it's ready to use as a child-sized "ice pack." It not only keeps the swelling down and slows bleeding, but it numbs the area and relieves the pain.

Achilles healed Pulling splinters from a squirming toddler's foot is an impossible task unless you dab on a bit of Baby Anbesol. After a thirty-second wait, needle and tweezer can be used to remove the offending object without a fuss. Apply peroxide and a bandage afterward.

Sting relief If your child is not *allergic* to bee or hornet stings, forget about using over-the-counter remedies to take the pain and itch away. All you need is Adolph's Meat Tenderizer. Rub it gently on the spot and it will draw the stinger up to the skin's surface and relieve some of the pain and itching as well. Getting a stinger out of a tender wound is the hardest part. Then soothe with a cool cloth. But if the swelling and redness are pronounced, and spreading to other areas of the body, and the child feels sick all over, get medical assistance. He may be allergic and need special medication.

Metal rashes Children's skin may be particularly sensitive. In fact, some children are even prone to rashes developed from contact with metal snaps on sleepers and other items of clothing. An easy solution to this common dermatological allergy is to cover the metal with fabric paint or snippets of a high-quality surgical tape.

Teaspoon of sugar makes the hiccups go away A spoonful of granulated sugar is an amazingly easy and effective (and easy to administer) cure for hiccups. Or give an older toddler a spoonful of creamy peanut butter. (Not for younger children, since peanut butter may get stuck in their throats.) Or try inserting a flexible straw, upside down, in a class of water. Hold the glass in your child's lap so she has to bend over to sip it. Encourage her to take a long drink.

Playing the role Your child may begin to have some fear of the doctor just about the time he is scheduled for the eighteen-month checkup. Buy a real stethoscope in a medical-supply store shortly before the appointment, and spend some time "examining" each other. Your child will become used to the instrument, and the appointment will go much more easily. Be sure to take the stethoscope along so your child can examine the pediatrician.

Sharing the pain If your child has to have blood drawn or any other uncomfortable procedure, encourage her to bring a stuffed toy "friend" to share the experience. If the doctor and nurse play along and Teddy gets the works—in the case of drawing blood, for example, treatment with the alcohol swab, needle stick, and Band-Aid—the experience may be less terrifying.

Medical notes It's a good idea to have a small notebook just for doctors' visits. You can make a note of weight and height (fun to refer back to as he grows), medications taken, immunizations received, various ailments and treatments over the years. Often you're asked to record on school and camp forms when a child had chicken pox, for example, and you can't remember; also, it's helpful to know what remedy worked, or to note a pattern of recurrent infections.

Helping the Medicine Go Down

There is nothing more frustrating than trying to get medicine into a child who won't comply. This stretches the limits of your imagination. Fortunately, you are not the only one to have faced this problem, and there are many solutions.

Tub treatment Liquid vitamins and some medicines can stain the baby's clothes, especially when the little one may spit it out, so why not administer those liquids while the baby is in the bath?

Smart medicine Administering medicine to infants in accurate doses, without spillage, is easy when you measure the correct amount and pour it into a bottle nipple, then let the baby suck. Leave the residue in the nipple, attach it to the bottle, and let your baby finish the dose with his formula or water. Try this right before mealtime, when your baby is hungry and willing to suck.

Pop artful If a child is particularly upset at the idea of taking a bad-tasting medicine, offer a lollipop to suck for a few minutes. When the mouth is full of that nice, sweet taste from the pop, the medicine will go down much more easily. Afterward, of course, have the child repop the pop right into her mouth.

Spoonful of medicine Sometimes the main problem in getting little children to take their medicine has to do with how it's offered. Though a syringe or dropper delivers the exact dosage and there are no spills, the sight of a syringe or dropper from the medicine bottle is a dead giveaway to a canny toddler that medicine is coming. In such a case, you may do better offering the medicine with a spoon. But measure the dosage into the spoon with the syringe.

Let them do it Children three to five years of age generally think they're ready for more self-control. The thought doesn't always translate successfully into admirable behavior, but taking medicine is a good place to start, and an oral syringe is the ideal instrument. Allow the child to help load it, pointing out that the dose has to be measured accurately. Demonstrate the proper technique on yourself first, with some water. Then allow the child to do it alone.

Rx for yucky medicines Mary Poppins, that magical, mythical Victorian nannie, recommended adding a spoonful of sugar to help the medicine go down. An even smoother solution is this modern approach. If your baby balks at taking medicine, give her an ice cube to suck on first. After she does so briefly, her throat will be numb and the medicine will slide down easily. Or precede medicine with a few teaspoons of crushed ice, ice cream, or frozen sherbet. Or crush approximately one tablespoon of frozen Popsicle or frozen fruit bar in a cup, add the prescribed dose of medicine, and spoon-feed the mixture. You may want to check with your pediatrician or pharmacist before trying this, since there are a few medicines that ought to be taken on an empty stomach. But many pediatricians agree that the important thing is to make sure the full dose gets into the child's system, and if a tablespoon of crushed frozen fruit bar helps do the trick, they're all for it.

Topping it off A few rainbow sprinkles on a spoonful of medicine may make it seem more palatable and shouldn't affect the effect of the medicine. If you want to be sure, ask your pharmacist.

Steamy solution A congested child isn't a prime candidate for dreamland, but turning your bathroom into a steam room can be a relaxing alternative or supplement to medication. Turn your hot shower tap on, close the bathroom door, and wait a few minutes until the room is filled with steam. Turn the shower off, wrap the baby in a light cloth blanket and take him inside. The steam will help clear his air passages and induce sleep. If your child is still congested in the morning, consult with your pediatrician.

Here's medicine in your eye Administering eye medicine can often be a struggle. Try doing it quickly when you're changing the child, just after you've laid him on the changing table. Sometimes you can administer the medicine before he realizes what's happened.

Sick in Bed

One mom fondly remembers her childhood illnesses as privileged moments. She was permitted to stay in her parents' large study-bedroom, which was the center of family life; she got to play with certain toys that were reserved just for illness; and she got to take her medicine with a spoonful of ice cream. She claims that having been so thoroughly indulged through her childhood illnesses got the need out of her system. As an adult, she almost never stays home ill in bed, so maybe her mom had the right idea. A child bedbound by chicken pox, flu, or other transient illness might be unusually grumpy but deserves some extra-special attention.

Bedside manners A bedridden child will appreciate having her favorite things neatly stored and readily available. A large muffin tin is ideal for holding small toys, old coins, a pair of dice, a balloon, animal crackers, crayons, a roll of adding-machine paper to draw on, a deck of flash cards, or a tiny picture book.

Chicken pox box A plain cardboard box that you paint white and cover with red dots and drawings of chickens—with lots of small favors inside—is the ideal gift for a child cooped up with the pox or flu. Fill the box with windup toys, coloring books, crayons, cookies, or stickers. Have a box ready for such needs because when your child gets sick there may not be time to go out and stock it.

Don't scratch it Remember to clip the nails of a child with chicken pox extra short. This reduces the danger of scratching and speading the disease during the incubation period, and it avoids scars or infections when the pockmarks begin healing.

Chill factor After getting up several times during the night to go downstairs to the refrigerator for special medicine, a smart parent got out the picnic cooler, packed the medicine in ice, and placed it next to the crib.

Liquid refresher When a child has diarrhea and is vomiting and can't keep food down but the doctor says to keep her drinking, fill an ice-cube tray with Gatorade and freeze. Wrap part of the ice cube in a washcloth and let the child suck on it. It won't prevent vomiting, but it will replenish fluids and potassium and help against dehydration. But take care: sports drinks are lower in calories and generally not as rich in nutrients as regular juice, and a dehydrated child needs all the calories and nutrition she can get.

Liquid dieting When children are on an all-liquid diet during the early part of a fever and you want a change from soda or sports drinks, offer gelatin dessert—mixed as a liquid and not jelled. At least there is some nutritional value in it, and a sick child might find it refreshing.

Marks of honor On the third or fourth day of the illness, a child with chicken pox is most uncomfortable. One way to help turn things around is to make a virtue of the disease. Have your child take an "inventory" of pockmarks—count what's on each arm, each leg, back and front of trunk, and so forth. It's easy to hit the one hundred mark—a badge of honor for your child to report to friends. A reward of one peanut, raisin, or M&M for each (rationed out over a number of days) is the icing on the cake, and buying bagfuls—and counting them out is another time filler. "Overall, this was worth about six baths with soothing additives," reports the father who suggested it.

Brushing Up: Dental Care

Dentists recommend wiping the gums of even young babies with a bit of gauze (check with yours to see just how to do it), and children should start brushing their teeth as soon as they are able. To help them understand how long they should brush, buy a small egg timer and let them watch the sand run through. To help them understand just how to brush, have them meet with your dentist. To help them be motivated to brush, you need the advice of other parents.

Cartoon helpers Buy a set of cartoon brushes—*Sesame Street* characters work just fine. Let the child select the brush, or character, he thinks will do the best job that day. Be imaginative. If the child is sulky, suggest that Big Bird is sulky today as well, so maybe Oscar could do a better job on his teeth.

Dental work If your child balks at toothbrushing, make it a chore that gets rewarded. Cut out a very large paper brush and award stars every time brushing is done properly. A mirror set at the child's height is a big help, and a timer (for an older child) helps him know how long to keep going.

Trading places When teaching your toddler to brush her teeth, give her your own toothbrush and let her brush your teeth. "You do me, and I'll do you."

Stepping up It's not easy hoisting toddlers up to sink level so they can see while they brush. Instead of spending money on footstools, tape together a few outdated phone directories with duct tape, then cover the top and sides with Contact paper (though not the bottom; paper is slippery) to suit the room's decor. The tape helps to give it a grip on the floor. Or cut and attach a small piece of rubber padding for the bottom.

Cuspid convenience When her kids resisted going "all the way upstairs" in order to brush after meals, one mother decided they had a point. It was time-consuming for them and for her as well, so she took advantage of a sink in a utility room off the kitchen, installed a toothbrush holder and bought an extra set of brushes, toothpaste, and cups. Now everyone brushes after meals—even mom.

Temper, Temper: When Tantrums Erupt

The other parent (or the genetic tendencies of the other parent's family) are usually blamed when a child has an explosive display of temper. Fact is, tantrums are an unpleasant but perfectly normal part of toddlerhood in any family, beginning typically at age two. What makes a difference is how parents deal with them.

Room service When your child has a tantrum, there's no reason you have to be a spectator to it. You can end it quickly and teach your child some self-discipline at the same time. As quietly as possible, tell your child that he is disturbing everyone with his behavior, but he is welcome to go into his room and let off steam for as long as he wishes. Without an audience, the tantrum usually comes to a halt fairly rapidly, and generally a subdued child will emerge from the room, ready for hugs and comforting.

Keeping your cool If you're having a hard time keeping your own temper in check in front of the baby, have a little talk with her instead. Make believe she's your best friend. She may not understand what you're trying to say, but she'll understand your tone of voice. The important thing is to keep all verbal communication on a rational level. Remember: your children learn from your example.

Learning by example If you want to teach a child how obnoxious—and silly—a tantrum can be, don't talk about it, demonstrate it. The next time your son or daughter starts to act up, join in: Stamp, kick the walls, lie down, and pound the floor. After his initial amazement, your child may realize how silly it looks, and as he gets older, realize that discussion is a more effective way to deal with an issue.

Time out for whom? When parents get frustrated with their three-year-old, they call a "time out" *from* her, letting her know her behavior is unacceptable. She gets the message, and an opportunity to regain her self-control.

Water cooler A fussy toddler will often calm down with water play, says a nursery-school headmistress we trust. A sinkful or bucketful will help but a bath is the best solution of all. If you pour a little baby shampoo in the bath, you'll have a bubble bath that's gentle, and no ring around the tub. A little food coloring in the tub will also amuse a child (and will *not* dye the skin unless you use a tremendous amount of it).

Word control After the tantrum is over, discuss with your child the possibility of selecting a secret word that brings it to a halt. She can pick the word herself. When a tantrum is next in the offing, try shouting out the word. The tantrum might just stop then and there.

Going to Potty

No matter how thrilled the child is who has become thoroughly toilet trained, her excitement pales next to that of her parents. Disposing of that last carton of diapers is one of the great moments of parenthood. Though parents may be more eager to begin the process than children, it shouldn't be rushed. We've seen a photograph in a book from years ago, when toilet training was instigated as early as six months: seated on top of the potty was the saddest-looking infant you can imagine. However, the fact that children with older siblings—whom they can emulate—catch on faster than only children indicates that the process can be encouraged. Not until you're a parent can you believe the candor with which playground parents share information on such private matters.

Bed-wetting To prevent bed-wetting and encourage more grown-up behavior, try waking your child up about four hours after he falls asleep and taking him to the bathroom. You may have to wake yourself for this chore, but it's probably worth setting your alarm until the bed-wetting phase is over.

Diapers away When toilet training starts, changing from disposable diapers to cloth diapers can make a difference. The change provides a transitional step, and some babies will find the change so unpleasant they'll gladly opt for the potty or the toilet.

Incentive programs Diaper training is quicker when little ones are promised cute lacy panties like mom wears or real he-man shorts like dad's.

Super bowl To ignite interest in toilet training, put a drop of red or blue food dye in the toilet bowl and challenge your little one to change it to orange or green.

Suiting up Make toilet training easier by using a bathing suit as a transition from diaper to underwear. This is especially useful for kids who resist wearing underwear during this period. Kids are usually thrilled to put on a bathing suit because it's associated with fun.

No time waisted Any elastic-waisted pants are good during toilet training, since they provide easy access in emergencies. You certainly don't want to deal with zippers or buttons during toilet training.

Potty à go-go Kids feel more at ease traveling when the comforts of home are available. Parents of toddlers in the middle of potty training who remember to bring the child's personal training potty along on car trips will be duly rewarded. Visits to grungy gas-station restrooms are avoided and the child will feel more secure and more encouraged if using the familiar setup.

O's and ah's When he's learning to use the toilet, your little boy can aim for the center of a floating Cheerio. If he hits the mark, you of course will be very complimentary.

Guiding light Be sure to leave a night light for your child to visit the bathroom, especially when you're away from home.

Out in the open It's easier to potty train during the summer months if you have a backyard. The potty itself can be kept outside and the child can wear bathing suits that are easy to get out of. Or, in the privacy of your own yard, he can go without any clothes.

Payoff list Is there a mother so pure she won't—finally—resort to bribery to help with toilet training? The guilty should be advised that everyone else is doing it. Appropriate bribes include stickers, gold stars, Gummi Bears, M&Ms (one for each success), candy kisses, real kisses, and pennies.

At first flush Some children like to flush the toilet, while others fear it (because part of them is being, and all of them might be, flushed away). If your child is among the latter, don't flush until the child has left the room.

Beyond the pail Just the right size (and price) for a portable potty—a plastic beach pail reserved just for this purpose. Use plastic bags for liners, of course.

Easy rider Sitting backward on the toilet may help your child feel more secure. Hands can grip the tank.

Portable potty The potty doesn't have to remain in the bathroom when a child is just getting trained. Take it from room to room and put it at the bedside at night.

Potty hygiene Packing a potty in the car for trips is fine, but what happens after it's used and disposal is the next problem? Answer: Line the potty with a small plastic garbage bag (don't forget the plastic tie) for hands-off cleanups between pit stops.

Peer training Peer pressure starts early, and it's not necessarily a negative influence. Toddlers at the onset of toilet training will benefit if parents arrange play dates with successful "trainees" who are around the same age. Teaching by example is the key here. Peer pressure does the rest.

Dry idea Don't give your child a drink before bedtime when potty training is in progress.

Bye-bye to Bottles, Security Blankets, and All That Stuff

Giving up the breast, the "blankey," and the pacifier are difficult for most children. What works best will depend on your own child's personality. While it may seem important to you at this point to have the child let go of a blanket or toy, the fact is that in the long run it doesn't matter if the process takes a little longer than you expected or might prefer. When the child is running for president, no one will remember when he or she gave up the bottle.

Doublespeak There's an almost irresistible urge to talk baby talk to pets and small children. When you're talking to your child, resist it. And see if you can persuade grandma to cooperate. Otherwise, the child has two languages to learn—baby talk and English. This is one case when being bilingual isn't helpful.

Straw man A small child—starting at nine months or so—can be trained to drink from something other than a nipple if you give him juice from a box with a straw. Squeeze the box gently as he sucks. He'll be drinking from a straw within three months.

Lap topper When you're ready to start weaning your child, set a rule that the child must be in your lap in order to drink from a bottle. Bottles are for babies, and babies don't walk. The thought of sacrificing their newfound freedom of mobility is usually enough to convert the most reluctant bottle babies to cups.

The bottle cup There once was a mother who found herself in a restaurant with a baby bottle but no nipple for it, and a baby who wanted milk right away. A waitress provided a glass of milk but baby wanted her ba-ba. In desperation, the mother poured the milk from the glass into the bottle, to see if baby would sip from it while mother held the bottle. Baby did. And she never went back to nipples again.

The juice solution If your toddler is used to drinking juice from a bottle, try diluting the bottle juice with more and more water, while occasionally offering him full-strength juice in a cup. Don't be surprised when he starts specifying "a cup of juice" instead.

Bottle refund If you want to take the no-more-bottle issue out of your hands, ask your doctor at the three-year checkup to urge the child to turn in all the bottles (and/or pacifiers) the following week and get a special prize in return for crossing such an important threshold.

D.Y.O.B. (discard your own bottle) Throw a bottle-tossing party. Talk about this big event—what you will serve, who will come. Wrap up a new cup as a present. The day of the party, round up all the bottles in the house ("hidden" by you in a few obvious places), take them to the trash, and throw them in, one by one. Then have the celebration. If the child later asks for a bottle, remind him they're gone. You may look to see if one has been forgotten—but it won't be found.

From breast to bottle Weaning will go easier on mother and child if one routine is replaced with another. If breast-feeding or bottles were offered just prior to nap time, read two books, listen to music, or sing baby a song instead. Whichever you choose, stick to it for three or four days before changing again. Babies appreciate routine.

Out of sight, out of mind Part 1 An overnight trip is a perfect occasion to wean children from bottles to cups. "Forget" to take the bottles. With a little luck, the bottle may soon be forgotten. Or do it on vacation. Since everything else is different, this is a good time for breaking habits. But in case your baby has a harder time with the change than you hoped, hide a bottle in your luggage.

Out of sight, out of mind Part 2 Similarly, a child returning home after some absence and busy getting reaquainted with the familiar bed, toys, and routines may not miss the bottle, pacifier, or blanket when it disappears. There are so many other familiar props available—toys, furniture, etc.—that the others may not be required for comfort.

Bribe idea To get a daughter to break a bad habit, such as thumb sucking, offer real nail polish as a bribe. Tell her once the little red lump on the top side of the thumb is gone, she'll have the polish of her choice, and offer to keep the nails polished as long as she doesn't backslide. (If she does, the process starts all over again.)

Winning cup Buy a special cup, in a special color, and wrap it specially for the child who's giving up the bottle. Buy a matching one for yourself so the two of you can have drinks together. Or give your child a bright-colored cup and tell him he can decorate it himself (with stickers) if he gives up the bottle. This has succeeded in instant weaning in at least one case.

The bottle fairy Round up all the bottles and tuck them out of sight. When your child awakens and asks for the first ba-ba of the day, gently explain that, when children reach a certain age, the bottle fairy comes during the night and collects big children's old bottles to give them to tiny little babies who really need them. This trick works best if the child has heard of the bottle fairy ahead of time (and the fairy is described as a symbol of growing up). After the visit, each time the child asks for a bottle, the myth of the bottle fairy is embellished with imaginative details regarding the fairy's dress or her jet-propelled diaper bag and the kindness she shows to new babies who can't handle cups as your big child does.

Slowly, by attrition Some mothers opt for a gradual reduction in the number of bottles available when bottle weaning begins. A "schedule" is helpful. Once a bottle is lost, strayed, or too worn to use, it's a goner, and make sure the toddler knows it. A gentle "Well, we don't have to worry about replacing it anymore, because you're getting too old for bottles" is enough to cover the action.

. . . Or all in a week Tell your child that the thumb sucking or the bottle habit can last one more week, and one week only.

Help the child mark time with a paper chain, removing a link each day. When the week is over, stick by your guns.

Donations, please Allowing children to "donate" or make gifts of their bottle(s) to younger siblings or a friend's new baby is a sweet and clever way to wean them from the bottle. Giving bottles to a smaller child makes the one who is graduating to a cup feel quite proud.

A matter of taste You haven't tried every trick in the book to wean a child off bottles if you haven't tried this one. If your older toddler is refusing to go off the bottle, "marinate" all the nipples overnight in grapefruit juice. Most children hate its sharp taste. When your child complains about how the nipples taste, tell him that's a sure sign that he's getting too old for nipples and bottles, but you have a remedy that will work—drinking from a cup.

Tub training If your little one is learning to drink from a cup, let her practice in the tub during her bath. She'll be able to drink—and spill—to her heart's content. And you'll have less cleaning up to do.

Bye-bye pacifier Before children are clearly too old for pacifiers and weaning becomes a problem, start the process by limiting pacifier use to bed and nap time. Then suggest that it's time to recycle the pacifiers for "little kids" who really need them. If you can wait, Christmas is a good excuse to have the child wrap the old pacifiers so Santa can spruce them up and redistribute them.

Toy holder Even after the pacifier stage is over, the handy holders that clip to a child's clothing on one side and have a snap or Velcro to hold the pacifier at the other end can be put to good use. Find a toy that hooks onto it and keep the baby amused while ensuring his toy won't land on the pavement, dirty store floor, or the floor of the car.

So long, security blanket The toddler was looking for her "blankey," and a grownup offered help. "What color is it?" "Blue and white," said the three-year-old. The beloved item, finally located, turned out to be a frayed collection of strings, totally unrecognizable as a blanket, and devoid of any color. The pandemonium that results when the item is misplaced—almost inevitably when you're rushing to get out of the house—is one reason parents are anxious to part the child from the "blankey." Another is the revolting sight of the dirty, stringy mass. One way to help speed up the separation process is to make the problem smaller—quite literally. Cut a patch from the blanket. You'll be surprised at how the part can substitute for the whole and delighted when your little one no longer drags the thing around, cleaning floors in the process. Some parents make the process gradual, chopping away at the blanket week by week.

Lullabies and Goodnights

Some lucky moms have kids who conk out at 8 P.M. but many wage a battle every bedtime. Some kids refuse to admit that they're ready for bed, though their eyes may be closing as they protest, while others are in need of calming down to make the transition from playtime to sleeptime. Classic bedtime stalls drive parents wild, including the one-more-story, I-need-a-glass-of-water, and please-stay-in-the-room-until-I'm-asleep syndromes. Hold your ground and look for help—in the form of advice from the playground.

Bedtime beat Bob Marley's brand of reggae music is credited with turning holy terrors into tranquil angels at bedtime. The reggae beat is very repetitious without being loud, boring, or irritating, and the melody has the effect of gentle waves on a Caribbean lagoon. But some parents prefer classical music, and others swear by New Age sounds, particularly ones that mesmerize with flutes, harps, and the sounds of nature (birds, waterfalls) mixed together. Wind chimes are also recommended, provided that a quick breeze won't stir them up and wake baby in the middle of the night.

Buzz off Most children, even when they're tired, balk at being told that it's bedtime. Instead of becoming the bad guy when you deliver the unwelcome announcement, disassociate yourself from the message. Set the timer, and tell your child that when it buzzes it's bedtime. No one can argue with a timer, and a power struggle is avoided.

Soft and warm For feeling cozy, relaxed, and warm at bedtime, there's nothing like soft, warm pajamas. Pop the pj's into a warm clothes drier for a few minutes. Run your hand around inside to make sure they're not too hot (hot metal snaps could burn baby's skin). Leaving a set of folded pj's on a radiator cover for ten minutes will produce the same effect. Again, check to see they're not *too* hot.

Low-tech night light Traditional night lights have two problems. One, they can't be controlled by the child (and some kids need the security of their own bedside lights), and two, they cast a light that makes shadows look like monsters. Bedside lamps for children are impractical, too. Children's rooms usually lack a night table. If they have lamps, they are sure to get knocked over during the first pillow toss. A perfectly simple, low-cost solution is available in the form of a utility lamp—an insulated rubber socket with a plastic cage around the bulb, a hanging hook, and an extra-long cord, the kind construction workers use. Hang it near the child's bed so the off-on switch is within reach. A pale pink, blue, or green 25- or 40-watt bulb is an essential part of this rig. When your child outgrows the need for the lamp, you'll find plenty of uses for the utility lamp in your basement, attic, garage, or deck. It can also be used as a bed lamp for encouraging reading when the child gets older.

Seascape The magic of shimmering light, a softly bubbling filter, and the languid motion of tropical fish make even the simplest aquarium a relaxing addition to your child's bedroom, especially after "lights out."

Fireside nap The gentle crackle and warm glow of a fireplace in a dimly lit room will also ease baby's path to sleep—unless the parent dozes off first.

Focusing in Counting sheep isn't an effective way to induce sleep if you're too young to count. But the purpose of such an exercise is to make you concentrate, and you can help even a small child do this by suggesting that she think very hard about something she'd like to dream about. This exercise will very often help your child relax and go quickly off to sleep.

Don't start what you can't finish Since children like routine, be forewarned. Anything you start as part of a routine may inspire a request for a nightly repeat, so don't start something you can't live with.

Tapering off You may have made a habit of sitting in your child's room until he drifted off to sleep, then regretted that decision and tried to reestablish the rules. But if your child is used to your presence, or fearful of going off to sleep alone, he may give you a hard time. One way to break the pattern is to say that you are leaving but you will be in to check very soon, and then abide by your word. Check in every half-minute the first night. Make the intervals slightly longer—a minute or so—the second night and slightly longer than that on the third. And so forth. Your child will be comforted, reassured, and relaxed enough to sleep. Within a few nights, you may find him peacefully off in dreamland by the first check.

Camping out in your room One solution to breaking a child's habit of crawling into the parental bed is to buy her a sleeping bag to keep in the master bedroom for late-night rambles. Tell the child three in a bed is too crowded, but it's okay to "camp out" in mommy and daddy's room.

Little by little Eventually, you'll want to discourage your child entirely from sleeping in your room, even in a sleeping bag. Do it with a seven-day program. Night 1 is spent inside your room, night 2 is spent at your door. By night 7, the child is in his own bed.

The big broadcast To help a little one get used to sleeping alone in a big bed or to make the transition out of the crib to a junior bed, take the nursery intercom monitor and reverse it. Let him listen to *you* so he doesn't feel so alone. Make sure you hum and sing so he hears you and talk a little, possibly mentioning his name ("What a good boy Alden was today") so he'll know he may be out of sight but not out of mind. Do this for ten minutes or so—no longer—then shut it off. Otherwise you'll always feel that "Little Brother" is listening.

Hall monitoring If your child wants you in the room as she's going to sleep, but you'd prefer to be involved in some other activity, a good compromise is to position yourself in the hallway outside her room, reading a book or performing another quiet activity. Reassure your child that you're a nearby presence and she'll relax and drift off to sleep; once she's stopped stirring, you can leave.

Pleasant dreams Many parents recommend reading Dr. Richard Ferber's book *Solve Your Child's Sleep Problems* before bedtime problems arise.

Inclined to sleep Is your baby restless at night because of a stuffed nose? One way to keep her more comfortable is by packing a blanket or pillow under the mattress beneath her head.

Freeze, pardner! If your child gets the heebie-jeebies at bedtime, telling him this tip was invented by another child may be enough to persuade him to try it. It goes like this: Lie on top of the covers and play Freeze—your eyes can be open or closed—but don't move a muscle. Stay that way for a minute or too, until you can't stand it anymore. Then, before you "thaw out," get under the covers, where it's far more relaxed and cozy—the ideal climate, in fact, for sleeping.

Primal dreams When you *and* the kids are too wound up for sleep, maybe one last blast of activity will help drain the excess energy. One parent calls this "letting it all hang out." Close the bedroom door, turn the lights low, and then vent your frustrations by pounding on, or screaming into, pillows, jumping up and down in one place, or just acting as silly as you can for five full minutes. Take it to the limit, set the timer, and bop around in a primal funk until you've exhausted whatever demons were keeping you from settling down for bed or a nap. This trick is especially handy after long trips or lengthy air travel across time zones that leaves you wired, not tired.

Monkey see, monkey do When their four-year-old son asked to keep a cup of water or juice next to his bed at night, his parents thought "why not?" Until his toddler sister demanded a cup for her crib. The solution? Each child received a bicycle water bottle, one with an attached cap that snaps on and off so even little sister can manage it. No spills in the crib, and no more demands for water in the middle of the night.

To warm the tummy Certain herbal or fruit teas (chamomile, fennel, apple), when sufficiently diluted (ten parts water to one part tea), make a soothing bedtime drink for children past the age where warm milk exclusively does the trick. Check with your pharmacist and pediatrician first to make sure there won't be unpleasant side effects you're unaware of. After sugared tea, teeth will need a brushing, of course.

Bedtime reading Books with fabric or cardboard pages are perfect complements to a toddler's bedtime routine since after you've read the story he may still not be wound down. Allow him to look at picture books by himself for a few minutes more. He learns to amuse himself and may find the activity relaxing—and sleep inducing.

Story tapes When kids beg for just one more story at bedtime, it's hard to resist their pleas. A compromise solution is to have a supply of commercially available story cassette tapes on hand. Better yet, record your own voice reading from their favorite books. A normal lights-out routine can be maintained while the children fall asleep listening to their favorite stories.

Monsters and Other Fears

Being placed in an adult-sized bathtub will alarm one toddler while another child may panic at the sound of a particularly noisy machine. Night-time fears are particularly distressing to both parent and child. Helping children adapt to the sights and sounds of the big world is one of the most frequently discussed topics in playgrounds or wherever parents gather to swap child-raising (or hair-raising) experiences. Paradoxically, childhood fears and the means to resolving them are both dependent upon the power of imagination—the child's and the parent's. The best tips we found for helping children to conquer their fears emphasize the importance of using fantasy play to turn the tables on all kinds of monsters—including roaring vacuum cleaners.

Acting out Playacting is a good way to act out fears of particular occasions (the first day of school, a visit to the doctor, an encounter with a neighborhood pet, etc.) and an excellent way for you to know what's on your child's mind. Provide props and enter into the game and you may not only alleviate the problem but also get to know your child better.

Pet peeves Children will be less fearful of pets if they have learned to deal with them in a way that won't inspire the animal to bark or be rough. Explain to your child that she must never, ever pet an animal without asking the owner's permission, since some dogs are afraid of being petted by strangers and may bark. Explain that the best way is to put your hand out palm up, to let the dog sniff it and know that you're trying to be friendly before you try to pet.

Trim trauma To lessen the trauma of a first haircut, have your child come to watch mom or dad (or an older sibling) have a haircut once or twice before the scissors are applied to his hair. Haircut shops that cater to children make the experience more pleasant. They know how to deal with young children and often have car-shaped barber chairs, giveaway lollipops, etc.

First cuts When your child is ready for a first haircut, remember to call it a "trim"—kids know "cuts" hurt! And bring an extra shirt, so the itchies can be held to a bare minimum. If you think your child will demand to be held during the cut, wear comfortable clothes.

A walk in dreamland Just saying "goodnight and pleasant dreams" isn't enough if your child is worried about bad dreams. The remedy is to encourage pleasant dreams. After lights out, "walk" your child through the kind of dream he'd prefer. Start with a few questions like "Where would you like your good dream to take place?" After you've rehearsed the good dream, tell him to keep his eyes closed and think through his pleasant dream step by step as he falls asleep.

Talking cure If a child thinks there are monsters in her bedroom, telling her that they don't exist, or that there aren't any at your house, won't ease her fears. Tell her instead that since monsters exist *only* in the imagination, you and she can use your imaginations to talk back to the monsters. Maybe they're frightened, too. Or they just might need a good scolding, from the child herself.

Monsters mashed When your child tells you there is a monster in his room and he is scared, remind him that it's his monster, he made it, and he can make it do anything he wants. Tell him to tell it to go away, and chances are he will. And it will!

A charming idea Bedtime fears and phobias go Poof! when mommy and daddy suddenly produce a decorative bowl of "magic powder" (scented talc with a fuzzy powder puff) and declare it to be the best talisman for warding off *whatever* the child fears most. Select a magic incantation ("Monster, be gone!") and, together, sprinkle a small amount around the corners of the child's bed. Works like a charm.

Love potion no. 5 A "magic" handkerchief (scented with mother's perfume) will also "send away the bad dreams" at bedtime.

Monster spray Here's another talisman that will rid your child's room of nighttime monsters. One mother calls it "Monstercide Spray." Fill an empty spray bottle with water and a dash of extract or oil (in a scent monsters hate), then label it and present it to your child. Suggest spraying everywhere. You may be surprised at how many monsters there are to vanquish and how many days it takes. But they'll be gone soon.

No trespassing If magic dust, magic spray, and magic powder don't do the trick, have your child make a sign: "No Monsters

Allowed!" Incorporating her own drawing of the monster into the sign could make a big difference.

Draw them away If your child has had a particularly terrifying dream (and remembers it), have him draw a picture of the dream. Tell him if he wants the dream gone, all he has to do is tear it up and throw it away when he's done. When the drawing goes, so goes the dream.

Abhorring a vacuum When a one-year-old girl became hysterically frightened of an especially large and loud vacuum cleaner, her mother played a game with the child's favorite doll (Ernie from *Sesame Street*). The mother let Ernie inspect the vacuum cleaner up close and then let him hop aboard for a ride while she worked. The daughter's not afraid anymore. She loves to watch Ernie take a vacuum ride.

Diversionary tactic If baby's afraid of the bathtub, find something that will distract him—it could be vinyl, stick-on letters, soap that you can use to "draw" with, a rubber ducky, or some other kind of toy that's reserved for tub time only. In his excitement to get to the toy, he may well forget his fear of the tub.

Finicky Eaters and Junk-Food Fanatics

Children who wallow in mud and delight in playing with a toy called "Slime" may suddenly become fastidious about their meal habits: they won't eat certain foods that are touching on the plate, resist anything that even looks "yucky" and complain that "We never have anything good." ("Good," of course, would be a meal consisting of french fries, soda, and Twinkies.) You've got two matters at issue: cutting down on the consumption of junk food and increasing the consumption of food that is nutritious. Battling over food is the last thing you want to do, because that creates all kinds of food problems (the child overeats or refuses to eat), so try to keep a level head and keep the skirmishes to a minimum. It helps to remember that a hungry child needn't be coerced to eat. If your child hasn't filled up on junk food, he'll eat at dinner. As for between-meals eating, remember that children (like adults) take the path of least resistance: if a healthful snack is there, that's what they'll eat.

Creating demand When you want your child to eat a certain food, don't offer it at first. Serve the regular baby food to the child while serving yourself a portion of the "special" food, being sure to mention how good it is as you eat it. The idea is to wait until the child *asks* for the food you're so obviously enjoying. This works best for toddlers, but older kids may fall for it, too.

Tray temptation Encouraging children to eat nutritious food isn't always easy and getting them to eat nutritious snacks may be especially difficult if junk foods are easily accessible. But if you anticipate their hunger at snack time with a plate of raw cut-up vegetables, crackers, raisins, and fruit, attractively arranged as if it were the centerpiece for a grown-up party, you'll be surprised at how quickly hungry youngsters will devour it, before it occurs to them to ask for cookies and chips.

Changing the course You'd have to be a child psychologist to figure this one out but it worked for one mother whose children refused to eat vegetables with their dinner. Instead of serving vegetables *with* dinner, she served them, piping hot, in a communal bowl, *before* dinner, while everyone was still watching television. No fanfare, just "Here's a snack before dinner, use your hands, just make sure they're washed first." Sharing from the same bowl appealed to the kids, and they were soon eating everything that was served—including Brussels sprouts.

Make it special Child psychology and reverse psychology are close cousins. The mere fact of placing limits on fruits and vegetables can be enough to get a child to eat them. Here's a sample script: "I have a surprise treat. You may have . . . three strawberries, one carrot, three Brussels sprouts, but that's all for now. No more until later." Why does it work? Ask a child psychologist.

All in the presentation Sometimes presentation is as important as the food itself. A child who isn't interested in eating the conventional cereal-and-fruit breakfast might be intrigued by a self-service selection that arrives in a cupcake pan—one section with berries, one with bananas, one with bits of cheese, the others with mixed cereals.

Shaped to suit Food that looks different is accepted differently. Using animal- or other-shaped cookie cutters may make sandwiches more appealing, particularly if the child is allowed to select a special shape—a duck, a bear, or a dinosaur.

Hands on Some hard-core finicky eaters will eat only finger foods. If they're healthful selections, so what? As long as you know your child is getting the proper nutrients, don't worry, serve it raw, cooked, off or on the bone—any way they'll eat it.

Mommy's helper When she can help you prepare the food, even the most finicky eater can sometimes be persuaded to taste or eat more. At three, many children have the skills for routine kitchen jobs: rolling meatballs, pulling husks off corn, pouring liquids from a small cup (which you've premeasured) into a bigger one. Be creative about the tools you let her use. For example, you can buy a small wooden paddle to use instead of a knife for spreading peanut butter, then put a dab of it on the edge of a plate rather than have her scoop it out of the (glass) jar. It may take a bit more time to do the job this way, but not only may you reduce eating problems, you'll also build the child's confidence about her "helping" skills.

Sweet trick Kids with a sweet tooth can be encouraged to eat low-sugar cereals with a simple compromise: allow them to top off the healthier, parent-approved breakfast cereal with a sprinkling of their own, high-sugar favorite.

Chef du jour Children need to feel they have a say in things, and one of the best ways parents can help fill this need is in planning meals. Even the most finicky eater will perk up and participate if you handle the menu planning wisely. Start by explaining to the child that everybody needs certain foods in order to grow. Then run down a list of foods from the major food groups and let the child pick one or two items from each category. Keep running through the list until you're both satisfied, write down the selections or have the child draw a list or cut out pictures from a magazine, then post it on the refrigerator door and stick to it.

Old foods, new styles If mealtime boredom is the problem, innovation is the solution. Try serving frozen foods without thawing them. Carrots, peas, and string beans are ideal finger foods suited to this purpose. Yes, they may sound yucky to you, but that may be exactly what makes them appealing to your child.

Grate idea If your child won't eat vegetables, you can sneak added nutrition into burgers, meatballs, and meat loaf by adding grated carrots, zucchini, or squash to your regular recipe. They won't change the flavor.

Natural soda Want a fruit drink that's less expensive and more healthful than the commercial punches and "cocktails"? Mix sparkling mineral water or plain seltzer—which doesn't have added salt like club soda—with fruit juice of any kind. Strong-flavored juices such as pineapple and grapefruit, if your child likes them, can be diluted particularly well.

Milk and juice pops Frozen juice pops are sometimes much more appealing to children than plain juice and good for sick children as well as for treats. Make two-tone pops or freeze a berry in the center of the cube for something special. Juice frozen in a small dixie cup is fine, too; no stick is required, just peel away the edge. Children who aren't getting enough milk can up their intake with calcium-enriched orange-juice pops or pops made of frozen chocolate milk.

Picky, picky Children who can be trusted to handle a toothpick safely will enjoy "hors d'oeuvres" of meatballs, pieces of fruit, and pieces of cheese—even vegetables that might not be appealing in some other form.

Taking (out) your lumps You may be surprised to discover that many children enjoy soup. You may be equally surprised (and less delighted) to discover that your child is one of the many who don't like anything *in* the soup. (These children may or may not be among the group that doesn't like pulp in their orange juice, either.) Since clear soup is pleasant as a first course but doesn't constitute what most of us think of as a full meal, try this solution: Put some of the chicken and vegetables, along with the broth, in the blender, purée them, and mix back into the soup. Most kids will accept a soup that's thicker, so long as it doesn't have any lumps.

Healthful and fun Have children help you shell the peas and trim the beans and they may be more disposed to eat the products of their labors. Also make healthful snacks appealing. Stuff an apple with peanut butter and cut horizontally in rounds. Or cook sweet potatoes, wrap them in napkins, cut off the tops, and tell children to squeeze and eat. Or stuff tube macaroni with peas and other vegetable bits.

Mealtime fun For a fussy or easily distracted eater, any meal is easier if it's turned into a picnic—in the yard, on the patio deck, or on a plastic table cover in the middle of the kitchen floor.

Moo juice Fill a nearly empty jam jar with milk, shake it up, and have a sweet treat.

Shake it up Make a nutritious gelatin dessert with unflavored gelatin and natural (no-sugar-added) juice.

Taster's choice Rules of thumb: to little ones, drinks taste better through a straw, soup tastes better from a cup, and food tastes better if it can be picked up rather than speared on a fork. Convert as many foods as possible into finger foods—skinny toast strips, cooked carrots cut in spears—and you may have fewer food fights.

I Can Dress Myself

As with all learning experiences, it's important for the parent to focus on the goal—you want your child to be able to get dressed without your help, don't you?—and not become derailed by the process. Like every other move toward independence, a child's effort to get dressed requires a lot of patience on the part of the parent, who can do it faster, better, and certainly more attractively. It requires a lot of tact and self-control on your part not to correct her at every step of the way. While what she's wearing may be buttoned wrong, worn inside out, and not match, you'll be rewarded by the wonderful smile of self-satisfaction on her face.

Taking turns When you're in a hurry but your child insists on dressing himself, play "taking turns." He does one button, you do the next. He ties one shoe, you tie the other. This spares hurt feelings and teaches the child the concept of taking turns and sharing.

Hay foot, straw foot How can you make sure your child is putting his shoe on the right foot? Drill sergeants in the Civil War used to teach raw recruits how to tell the difference between their left and right feet by tying a hank of straw around one leg and a hank of hay around the other. Today's kids would probably not know the difference between hay and straw (and, we suspect, neither would their parents). What does work is this: Using a permanent marking pen, make two large colored dots on the inner edge of the sole of each of the child's shoes, about an inch below where the big toe rests. Tell the child to match the dots before putting the shoes on.

Telling back from front When your child is ready to help herself get dressed, mark the inside front of her pants with permanent marker. You can use a plain black laundry marker, but it's more exciting if you find a box of colored fabric markers and let the child pick her favorite color. If the child knows that she has to match the mark with her belly button, she'll put the pants on the right way.

Button up! When teaching small children how to button their clothes always remind them to start from the bottom and button *up*. They'll be able to see and match the corresponding holes and buttons so there's less room for error.

Keep it simple When children are old enough to start pulling on tops and bottoms by themselves, don't expect them to have a fashion sense as well. You can help at this stage by limiting choices—"The red pants or the blue pants?" *Never* ask, "What do you want to wear?" Your child usually hasn't a clue. Or you may have one of the kids who mull over an entire wardrobe, picking and choosing, then changing their minds. Don't lose control of the situation.

Dressed for speed Having a child dawdle when he's supposed to be dressing himself is no fun. But turning the dressing chore into a fast-paced race, with parent and child competing to see who finishes first, is a lot of fun for everyone. You can start with an "underwear" race, proceed to a top-and-bottom race, a sitting-down sock "hop," and finally, the ultimate—the shoelace race. Make sure the child wins enough times to make it fun. Daddy and mommy can slow down their own dressing by making enough silly mistakes to give the child a chuckle—and an edge.

Coat trick Here's a trick most every nursery-school teacher knows. Teach a young child to put her coat on by herself by laying the coat on the floor in front of her with the hood or neck at her feet. Tell her to bend over and put both arms into the sleeves, then flip the jacket up and over, and wow! she's dressed for outdoors. The first few tries are sometimes more fun than effective, but it works—because it's fun.

Ready—or not? If your child is a slowpoke about getting dressed, challenge his sense of competition. Set the kitchen timer for five minutes and have him beat the clock. Or use a stopwatch and have him try for a "personal best."

Touch control Toddlers who cannot yet lace their own shoes might like sneakers and shoes with Velcro straps until they're old enough to tie a bow.

Dressing smart Here's a great way to help kids learn how to dress themselves in clothes that don't clash. Buy all their tops in solid colors and buy patterns, plaids, or stripes for the bottoms.

With a little extra effort, you can buy compatible colors so any combination of top and bottom will match.

Ensemble dressing Stacking clothes in matching sets (socks, undies, pants, and shirt) so children can dress themselves without help is a popular tip, but you needn't stack the entire wardrobe that way. You'll do well enough to set aside one set of clothes in a special place (an old Easter basket?) every night at bedtime so they're ready to be put on in the morning.

On the button Often your child's idea of what looks good is the brightest clothing in the closet, preferably worn all at once. If you take some pride in having a well-dressed child and can't bear looking at the outfits she selects for herself, make up a large button that says, "I dressed myself today." Everyone will understand and your youngster will wear the button as her badge of honor.

Out to Eat

Children, it used to be said, should be seen and not heard, though years ago, at restaurants, neither was true. That has changed. America's favorite pastime is going out to eat, and 43 percent of every food dollar is spent dining out. Naturally, children come along. While it is unreasonable to expect fine dining with children in tow—they are physically incapable of sitting at the table as long as you can—with a certain amount of planning ahead both you and they should look forward to and enjoy the experience of visiting a restaurant.

A belt before dinner Although most restaurants will have a baby seat, many won't have the kind with a "seat belt"–type strap to keep baby from sliding out. If your traveling diaper bag has the room, find the largest old belt you can and stick it in there. You won't believe how often it comes in handy.

Stacked up If there are no high chairs in the fast-food court you're visiting, but there are stackable chairs, try stacking a few to get a chair that's high enough for your little one. The belt you carry (see the last tip) to keep the child in place in just such situations puts you ahead of the game.

A chair of one's own Those portable, collapsible seats are terrifically helpful when dining out or sitting at a friend's table. Make sure that the one you buy is designed so that it fits easily under most tables—take it home and try it on your own, for starters, before you remove the tags.

Sharing snacks Taking along a bag of snacks (dry cereal, animal crackers) to the playground is always a good idea, but dividing the snack into two or more plastic bags is even better. It allows you to parcel out the snack supply, and you're equipped to share with other children should the need arise.

Cheerio, young chap Finger food for baby satisfies hunger but it's equally important as a diversion. Keep a clean 35mm film container full of Cheerios. It will hold enough to amuse a six-month-old infant while his companions enjoy snacks of a more substantial sort.

Fun supplies If you dine out or make long car trips often, pack a kit of items to leave in the trunk so they are available to haul out when your child becomes restless in the restaurant or in the car. Include any or all of the following, depending on your child's age and interests: paper, a coloring book, crayons, markers or pencils, a story book, stickers, Silly Putty, a comic book, puzzle and maze books, tape and cassette, headsets, a small doll, or an action figure.

Photo play A small photo album with pictures of friends, relatives, pets, etc. will keep a little one distracted in a restaurant.

Or give the child a wallet filled with photos, play money, cards, and other things to look at.

Hunger appeasers Some parents know their child can't be counted on to stay in his seat for more than a one-course restaurant meal. But even if your child can sit for longer periods, when the appetizers come out of the restaurant kitchen and there's nothing on the tray for him, he may find it very difficult to remain patient. Ask the waiter to bring the child's main dish when the other first courses are served. Or see if you can get some melba toast or saltine crackers.

Table d'toy A small child in a restaurant is inevitably ready to leave when you're midway through the main course. To occupy her while you finish your meal in peace, bring along a "restaurant bag" of toys—a couple of small character figures, a windup toy, an activity or coloring book, a few crayons. Make these "restaurant only" toys so that they hold her interest and are something for her to look forward to.

Whine or dine The first time a child trashes a restaurant table—the sugar bowl is usually the first thing to go—the problem can be chalked up to inexperience. The second time, you have to take the blame. It's not enough to move ashtrays, water goblets, flowers, salt and pepper shakers, milk pitchers, and sugar packets out of the child's reach. Place them on an empty chair or have the waitress remove them from view. Out of sight, out of mind.

Spill insurance Don't throw away the carrying trays for soda pop from fast-food restaurants. Use them to hold soda or juice cans from the kitchen to the backyard or as a caddy for baby bottles when you're on the go.

Mall Trips and Small Trips

When you have kids in tow, a short excursion can be fun for all or it can turn into a rushed and totally exhausting experience. Our contributors seem to have most of the bases covered when it comes to thinking up ways to get around problems on short hops, whether it's visiting a store or spending a day at the beach.

Lock up When your little girl gets antsy at a shopping center and wants to stroll on her own two feet, carrying the folded stroller is awkward and uncomfortable, especially in a crowded store. You can leave it unattended but secure if you get a small cable-type bicycle lock—the kind that has a combination, not a key. (Then you can write the combination under the seat in case you or a babysitter forgets it.) Just lock the stroller to a tree or a pole and stroll away, knowing it will be there when you get back.

Strollman If your toddler refuses to sit in the stroller and wants to walk or be carried instead, try putting his cassette player into the stroller with him. Often a bit of entertaining music is distracting enough to keep him in his place.

Sur la plage Pack extra beach towels for use only when traveling to and from the beach. They'll keep little bottoms cool on the way and the car seats dry coming home.

True grit Getting little ones clean, dry, and free of sand before leaving the beach can be a real chore, especially when there are no showers and you're running late. And riding home in a scratchy, sandy bathing suit isn't fun for kids or good for your car's upholstery or carpeting. Try this quick and painless method: Bring a large can of talcum powder or talc mixed with cornstarch and sprinkle it liberally over the wet, sandy areas of your child's body. The talc or cornstarch will absorb moisture and sand will brush off more easily. Treat tiny feet even more gently by talcing and brushing them with a dry cotton terrycloth towel rather than your bare hands.

Toddler pool When going to the beach with a very small child, carry an inflatable pool to put right next to your beach blanket or chair. Pour in a few buckets of sea water and the child can frolic without your worrying about her being at the water's edge.

Sun protection Putting sunscreen on your little one's face may be a battle. Try putting some on the child's finger and persuade him to do your nose and cheeks while you do the job for him. You'll reduce the amount of fussing—and the job will go more quickly.

Shady business Keep a spare pair or two of children's sunglasses in the glove compartment of the car. Though they're often forgotten at home, they're very nice to have if the day is painfully bright.

Keeper of the belts If your little one rants and raves every time she's asked to get into her car seat, try assigning her a "very, very important job," a request that kids of a certain age find hard to ignore. Tell her the trip can't start until she personally takes charge to make sure everyone else aboard is securely buckled into their seat belts. If a sibling balks at this transfer of authority, put the sibling in charge of making sure the *doors* are locked.

Shady days Make a sunshade for the rear-facing infant car seat with a handle. Cut a crib sheet in half and sew elastic to the cut-off edge. Pull the carrying handle of the car seat straight up and stretch the sheet over it and down the back. It's not as fancy as the store-bought kind, but it's a money saver and it works. Personalize it with T-shirt paint if you wish.

Settling in As you well know, it's critical to have all the children strapped into their car seats. Raise their awareness of the need for seat belts by involving them in a routine. Tell them that the car key does not work until everyone is strapped in. They'll urge one another to complete the task so that takeoff is not delayed. What's nicest about establishing this routine is that if you forget to remind them about seat belts, chances are that they'll remember to remind one another—and you.

Taking turns Changing the kids' seating arrangements on daily car trips will put an end to squabbles over who sits where. Just remember to keep a chart *in the car* to settle arguments *before* they start.

Ouch! A couple of reusable cold packs will take the heat off hot buckles on car seats and safety belts on summer days.

Bring a towel A cotton towel will absorb perspiration in the car seat under the baby. You may have to cut holes in it to slip the straps through. When you remove the baby, leave the towel on top of the seat to keep the metal portions of the belt from overheating while you're gone.

On the Road Again: Car Tricks

Some people think hell is a place where you're sent on an eternal car trip with a lot of children and rest stops spaced at hundred-mile intervals. Keeping children entertained and calm, fed and comfortable—and the driver unruffled—during long car journeys is very much on the minds of the playground parents.

Dangle it Give a toddler a toy to play with when she's in a car seat and you'll be picking the toy up from the floor at every stoplight. Instead, attach a crib toy to an elastic string and fasten the string to the car's sun visor. Experiment a bit to find a toy that comes easily within the child's grasp. If the elastic doesn't work, use a set of plastic links instead.

Juice à go-go Freeze boxes or canteens of juice ahead of time if you're planning a long trip so they'll still be cold when your little guy gets thirsty. (Give him a drink just before you leave the house so the juice box can be saved for a while.)

Power source For longer trips when you need a warm bottle, buy a bottle warmer that can be plugged directly into your car lighter.

Rear views Drape a play blanket (one with a *Sesame Street* or Walt Disney motif) over the backseat of the car so your infant has something to look at and kick at on car rides. Or use one of those cloth mats with a mirror, squeak toy, teether, etc. attached to it. It will come in handy for a baby who is too old to sleep through a whole trip but too small to be facing front. (Babies who weigh under seventeen pounds must face the backseat.) Take the blanket with you on trips and it also becomes a great entertainment center in hotel rooms.

Emergency compartment Even the best-organized mom may inadvertently leave the diaper bag at home. Stow a disposable diaper and a small quantity of wipes in the glove compartment of your car for just such occasions. Put them in an airtight bag, so they won't lose moisture.

Facing up One of the best things to take on a long trip is a sticker book of faces with press-on noses, ears, etc. These have so many pieces one can keep a child occupied for hours.

Stickups Colorforms work on automobile (and airplane) windows.

Little by little If you're packing a toy bag or a bag of surprises to keep children entertained on the road, dole the goodies out slowly. Don't toss the whole lot in the backseat at once or kids will tear into them and then quickly tire of the lot. If you can't keep the treats hidden in your bag, wrap them separately (ordinary brown paper will do; the point is camouflage) and set a milestone (mileage or time passed) before another surprise will be doled out.

Travel games Long car trips can be boring for children of all ages, no matter how many toys or treats you've brought to entertain them. Since the world rushing by outside should be a distraction, why not use it? Play road games pegged to the passing scene. "Let's see who'll be first to see a brown cow." No cows? Try making sentences from letters on license plates. The geography game is fun and a great way to learn. The last letter in the name of the state or town you're rolling through becomes the first letter of the next place name. You're in Arizona? Alabama leads to Arkansas, then Sacramento. "Who'll think of the next one? C'mon, it begins with O." Older kids love this game and can keep it up for miles. Younger children whose geography knowledge is limited can enjoy playing with names of foods. Or ask them to hunt for letters of the alphabet, one at a time, in road signs. (They may go for miles waiting for a Q to show up.)

Road stops Here are a few ways to break up a long trip:

- Stop at a pet store and look at the animals.
- Go through an automated car wash and watch the brushes swirl around you.
- Stop at a small local airport and look at the airplanes take off and land.
- Stop at a post office and buy a few colorful one-, two-, or three-cent stamps to play with.

Away for the Night

After your first few nights or weekends away with your child, you'll probably get into the routine of it and manage to remember everything you should have packed. Making a master list that you photocopy and take out each time is a big help. What also helps is a wonderful sense of humor and the ability to go with the flow and improvise—to make a crib where there is none, for example.

Hotel cribs Don't ever hesitate to take your infant on an overnight trip just because you have to stay in a hotel. Drawers in hotel bureaus are large enough to double as cribs for the largest baby. Bring a mattress pad, baby pillow, and liner from home. Place the drawer on the floor and line it with a folded hotel blanket that covers all the rough surfaces, add your linens from home, and top them off with a hotel sheet and your baby's travel blanket.

For floating off to sleep No cribs in the hotel? And you think a bureau drawer will be too hard for the baby to sleep in? An alternative possibility is an inflatable plastic wading pool. It packs neatly, and once it's blown up it makes a soft-sided crib—and not a bad playpen, either.

For warming, it's cool That ice bucket you may never have needed before will come in handy once you have an infant. It's not just a cooler; it's also a warmer. Fill it with hot water, then place the bottles inside. They're ready in minutes.

Meeting out-of-town relatives If you're off to visit relatives your children have never seen before, put together a small photo album so the kids will have some idea of who's who when they get there. Nothing's worse than driving five hundred miles to spend a few days with Aunt Joan and Uncle Brad and having your youngest hiding in her parents' shadow throughout the entire visit.

Clothes storage For a trip to a cabin in the woods, one mother packed her four-month-old son's clothes in a ten-gallon square Rubbermaid container with a lid on it. The airtight container kept moisture out, doubled as a bassinet, and tripled as a toy box and carry-all when they went to the beach. She used it as a storage box when vacation was over.

Medicine bag When you're packing for a trip, don't forget to take along a first-aid kit of items that are just for your child. Obviously these will vary depending on the time of year and place you are visiting. Will there be mosquitoes? Is the weather likely to cause chapped lips? It will also depend on the odds that there will be a pharmacy nearby open at all hours. The kit might include a thermometer, petroleum jelly, nonaspirin pain reliever (and a special spoon to administer it), allergy reliever, first-aid cream, ipecac, decongestant/antihistamine, bandages, a nose aspirator (to relieve clogged noses in little babies), and any prescription drugs.

Shirt off your back To help put an infant to sleep in an unfamiliar bed (portable crib, host's house), instead of sheets use one of mom's worn shirts. The familiar smell and touch reaffirms mom's presence and relieves any anxieties.

Travel safety If your crawler or toddler is going to be stuck in a hotel room or guest house for any length of time during a trip, remember to pack some electrical tape for covering the wall outlets. It's handy to secure any childproofing wads of tissue (or shoulder pads) on sharp table edges as well.

Packed to suit Traveling with children is much easier when everyone has her or his own bag, and a say as to what's inside. After clothes and essentials are packed, let the child select what toys to take. If there's no room in the suitcase for anything but clothes, a separate carrying case for toys may be in order. A plastic lunch box is a fine tote for limited space such as a crowded car or airplane seat. If you have the room, a guitar case is a child's idea of a great suitcase. Or use a duffel bag, backpack, or any other kind of bag of the child's choice. The assortment of things that she considers necessities may seem bizarre to you, but remember that what you see as a stick and a stone is a wand and magic rock to her. It's what she really wants to play with. The child is in charge of packing it and making sure nothing gets lost.

A tape in time When visiting relatives or friends who don't have children, make sure you bring along plenty of toys. If there's a portable tape recorder and video player at your destination, bring music and a video tape your child will enjoy. This is the perfect occasion for presenting that special tape your child has been asking for.

Traveling gear If you will be making frequent weekend (or longer) trips with your child, get a small plastic bag and outfit it with toiletries—baby shampoo, baby oil, toothbrush, toothpaste, hairbrush—as well as first-aid items and baby aspirin, allergy medications, Dramamine or other motion-sickness medication, even an airplane sickness bag. It'll be ready to go in a jiffy and you won't have left anything behind.

Bagged for speed The most efficient method for packing clothes is to sort and stack the child's wardrobe into daily, coordinated outfits—pants and a shirt that complement each other on the bottom, socks and underwear on top. Tie each group with a ribbon or secure it with a large rubber band. Some piles can be put together to reflect special occasions, such as a rainy day or a trip to a fancy restaurant. This method cuts out time-consuming rummaging around in bottomless suitcases and ensures that clothes that make up an outfit will be worn together, and it keeps the clothes looking almost freshly pressed. As your child gets older and can dress himself, he'll be able to handle the task a lot more efficiently if he can deal with only one separate stack of clothing at a time.

Travel tips Before going on any kind of trip—anything from a small junket to the doctor's office to a major journey abroad—tell the children (even two- and three-year-olds) where you're going, how you're getting there, what's expected of them along the way, and some of the things you'll all be doing when you arrive. If this is done routinely, they will have a better idea of what's happening and will probably be more cooperative.

Mommy, what's that? Gift wrapping even the smallest item makes it special, and this is especially true on long trips whenever boredom sets in. A coloring book, book of mazes, connect-the-dots, crayons, or Silly Putty are all made extra appealing if wrapped with a bit of colored paper and a ribbon.

Into the Wild Blue Yonder, Kids and All

Air travel can be relaxing, even with children—*if you plan ahead.* If your child hasn't flown before but is old enough to comprehend, explain as much as you can to her about airports, airplanes, pilots, flight attendants, inflight movies, music—and the wonderful food brought right to her seat. Books that describe an airplane trip help prepare your child also. After she's briefed, it's time for you to fine-tune your packing list, because there are things a child needs before she can fly that Peter Pan never dreamed of. These are practical tips from the playground to get you off the ground with your sanity intact.

Ascents and descents When traveling by air with infants, make sure baby has something to suck on during landing and takeoff and whenever else you know a change of altitude is underway. Any clean, wet cloth will do, and so will a nipple, by itself or attached to a bottle of milk or juice. If all else fails, use your own clean finger. Older children should always have straws, and a bottle, box, or plastic container of their favorite beverage on hand, so they can take small sips during takeoff and final descent, when ear-popping is most prevalent. Fellow passengers will appreciate your preparing the children. Sipping or sucking leads to swallowing, which helps keep ear passages clear, thus preventing painful pressure on tiny eardrums, which may set off loud wailing that always sounds louder and more annoying in the confines of an airplane cabin. Lollipops and sugarless gum can help in this regard if the child is old enough. Just make sure children keep swallowing. (Buy gum before you get to the airport, since some airports don't stock it because uncaring passengers leave it behind, stuck under seats or in ashtrays where it's hard to remove.) An alternative way to handle this is with a children's decongestant, such as Dimetapp. It should be taken before boarding; ask your pediatrician for specifics and recommendations.

Bicoastal bedtime Night flights are best when traveling with young children, especially when you're heading west to east. The "red eye" from California to New York is particularly conducive to sleep.

Boarding party If you have the option of having two adults in attendance while traveling by air, have one of them board the plane as early as possible with all carry-on baggage, food, drink, car seats, etc. The second adult stays behind in the waiting area and keeps the child, or children, occupied until the last possible moment before boarding. By that time, everyone's in his seat, kids aren't jostled in the aisles, and when you reach your assigned seats, you've only to sit down, fasten your seat belts, and sit back for takeoff.

Take a break If takeoffs and landings aren't a problem for your child, don't always opt for a direct flight. Flights that involve stops make sense for a couple of reasons: they're usually less expensive, and on long trips your child will welcome a break and the opportunity to run around a little. Things may be too complicated if you have to change airlines (there's always the luggage problem), but brief layovers can be a boon.

Kids' meal Some airlines offer children's meals that can be special-ordered in advance of takeoff.

Hoist your cups aloft Those flimsy plastic tumblers used for drinks on airplanes were not made for tiny hands. So pack a plastic cup with its own cover if you're traveling with a child. Flight attendants will gladly pour milk or juice into your child's cup.

What's French for "skippy peanut butter"? Traveling overseas, you can find diapers, baby food, and even formula, but you may not have success finding special brands of food for an older child, such as a favorite cereal, cracker, or type of peanut butter. If your child is a finicky eater who happens to be addicted to one of these, take them along for the sake of both parent and child.

Traveling en famille If you're traveling with children by train in Europe, alert your reservations agent that you're going as a group. Many rail systems have special family compartments that are shared with other families. It's a wonderful way to meet people, the kids love it, and it's easier on you and the other passengers.

Zoned out If you have taken an overnight flight, no matter how wakeful everyone may feel on arrival, insist that everyone (even the grownups) take a nap immediately after getting to wherever you will stay. If you wake up late in the afternoon, go out to dinner, and have a reasonably early bedtime, you will get back onto a normal schedule quickly and reduce the jet-lag problem.

Taking no chances Before going away on an extended trip, ask your pediatrician if he can recommend a pediatrician (and/or a hospital) in the town you're visiting. If you need a pediatrician while traveling abroad, the very first place to call is the nearest United States embassy or consulate. Usually it can provide you with a list of English-speaking doctors, and many foreign-service staffers have children of their own, so you're likely to have another parents' recommendation as reassurance.

Keeping your powder dry If you travel to a remote area or simply a foreign country with a child who is prone to ear infections, don't spoil your vacation searching for a doctor to prescribe suitable medication and a druggist to fill the prescription. Before traveling, ask your pediatrician for a prescription for an antibiotic that comes in powdered form (Amoxicillin is one) and doesn't require refrigeration. Fill the prescription before leaving and make sure it's packed in your carry-on luggage, not in the checked baggage. The medicine won't do you any good if your luggage (with it inside) gets diverted to Tangier and you're landing in Greece.

Getting Yourself (and Your Child) Organized

Young children create more mess than they can clean up by themselves, but both of you can work at being organized if you have the right storage solutions. Look around the notions and housewares departments and closet shops for storage ideas that will help you keep things as uncluttered as possible. Put things where they are convenient; that seems obvious, but requires some forethought. For example, don't put anything behind something else if it will be used often. And see how you can expand the space you already have. If you have lots of air space between shelves, for example, build another shelf or add another level of shelf spaces by buying a vinyl-coated metal rack or below-shelf basket.

Giveaways When your child puts on an item of clothing that no longer fits, that's the time to discard it. But where do you put it?

Hang a laundry bag just for discards in the closet, and you can collect them as they accumulate. When the bag's full, sort and store them.

Handled with care Your little kid at a certain age may wind up with lots of "swords" and other long-handled toys. The best container—a wastepaper basket.

Off the rack Shelves are actually more useful than hanging space for children's clothes until they are near-adult height. Put shelves in the closet instead of hangers.

Locker-room tactics Old gym lockers can be bought, painted, and used for special storage closets. Great for sports equipment, etc.

Rake them in The fastest way to gather up baby's toys—a lawn rake.

Clearly the best Clear, inexpensive, see-through plastic shoe boxes make ideal containers for tots' tiny toys, especially Legos or Playmobil items. Since the boxes are transparent, a youngster will have no trouble selecting toys without adult help. Just make sure the boxes are on a low shelf so she can easily reach in.

Getting pegged Kids will be much more likely to hang up jackets and caps if there are pegs or hooks at their level, either in their rooms or near the back door.

Box storage Keep a large laundry basket (or large cardboard box—empty TV, air conditioner, or personal-computer cartons are ideal) as a repository for stray toys. The box is easily moved to the children's room if company calls or you can't stand the mess any longer. Go through the contents at least once a week and let the kids help sort the toys out and return them to their usual storage spots. Otherwise, you'll soon need a bigger box.

Lots of boxes Lots of toys require lots of picking up. Try putting toys in half a dozen different boxes and make a rule that only one box at a time can be used for play. Let the kids stock each box themselves, but once they're bored with one, it goes back into place before a new one comes out.

Carry-all cartons Half-gallon milk or juice cartons with handles make great carriers for toddlers' small toys. Cut the tops off below the caps, at a point where little fingers can reach in but toys won't tumble out. The lighter plastic cartons can be cut with scissors. Heavier plastic will require a hacksaw. You might want to sandpaper the rough edges. Don't cut too close to the handle, which is the feature your child will appreciate most.

Toddler time management When you begin daily chores, let your toddler's travels determine the order in which rooms get spruced up. If he's in the kitchen, do that room first. If he's playing in the bath, that's the most efficient time to clean sinks and bowls. As the toddler moves, so do you. A plastic garden tray with a carry handle filled with a variety of cleaning supplies gives you mobility and flexibility in terms of which chores you'll do.

Label consciousness Even a preschooler can learn to be tidy. Label her drawers or plastic storage boxes with pictures of what should go inside them. Use labels from the boxes, or let an older child draw a picture to identify each box or drawers. (If she's drawn the picture herself, she'll know exactly what it's meant to be. Whether you will is another story.)

Backup information If your child is a puzzle fan, you may find yourself with tens, then dozens, then hundreds of pieces to keep track of. When they get mixed up with one another, sorting them out becomes a hopeless task. Prevent the problem by giving each new puzzle a letter, number, or color code the minute the box is opened, and code each piece immediately. "Lost" pieces are quickly matched with their mates.

Picture perfect Children often don't remember how their room looked when it was "neat and tidy." Try cleaning your child's room with your child helping, then take a picture of each part of the room to show how the bed, closet floor, underneath the bed, toy box, etc. should look when everything's neat and tidy. Post the pictures in your child's room at his eye level for reference. He will know what you mean when you ask him to tidy up.

Basket roundup Keep a bright-colored wicker basket or laundry basket in every room your children play in. They're the best way to make a hasty cleanup. Don't buy a basket with holes that are too large, though, since small toys will fall through.

Oh, the Things We'll Do and the Places We'll Go

Definition of a really great mom: someone who doesn't run out of play ideas when it's been raining for four days in a row. We're not sure that mom really exists—but some of the ideas playground moms swap most eagerly are those for keeping the kids occupied and entertained, both indoors and out.

Box art Make and design jewelry boxes and toy boxes using glue, pieces of fabric, macaroni, glitter, stickers, ribbons and bows, and buttons.

Makeup magic For Halloween costuming or regular dress-up you can powder hair to make it look gray, make a cotton beard and stick it to the face with corn syrup, and make "greasepaint" by combining one tablespoon cold cream, two teaspoons corn-starch, a teaspoon of water, and a few drops of food coloring.

Free play It's your child's job to explore the environment, not swell the coffers of the toy companies, one mother reminds us. In addition to the child's own toys, allow him to play with items you have left around specifically to be examined: magazines to "read," pots to bang. Have a toy box in each room to toss the items into in order to keep the house manageably neat.

On the mat Your child can make a set of two or four placemats to give to grandma as a present or to decorate the family dinner table. Make a collage of several small drawings or use just one large one, sandwiched between clear Contact paper.

Pantry crafts Necklaces, bracelets, and ankle bracelets can be fashioned out of macaroni, Cheerios, and multicolored buttons.

Cardboard creations Shoe boxes make a train; an empty wine or liquor case from the liquor store (with all its compartments) makes a car garage; old wallpaper books make paper-doll dresses and collage papers.

Recipes for fun

- *Homemade paint* Mix equal amounts of liquid detergent or liquid laundry starch with food coloring.
- *Homemade bakers' clay dough* Combine 4 cups unsifted flour, 1 cup salt, and 1½ cups water. Knead for 4 to 6 minutes. Cut with cookie cutters or shape and decorate with cloves, peppercorns, popcorn kernels, dried peas and beans. Bake at 350 degrees for 15 minutes or longer (up to an hour), depending on the thickness of the objects.
- *Homemade play dough* Blend until smooth 1 cup cornstarch and 2 cups baking soda with 1¼ cups water (plus a few drops of food coloring). Cook over medium heat, stirring constantly. Boil 1 minute until it's the consistency of mashed

potatoes and easily pulls away from the sides of the pan. Turn it out onto a cookie sheet and cool for several minutes, then knead until smooth. Molded objects left overnight will harden. Use this play dough to make beads, bracelets, etc.

- *Homemade bubble mixture* Mix 1 teaspoon Joy or an other liquid detergent and ¼ cup water.
- *Homemade bubble blowers* Use two twist ties (one for the "head" and the other for the handle) or cut out the bottom of a small paper cup. Dip one end in the mix and blow through the other.

Crafts center Keep a drawer or plastic bin full of items such as stickers, glue, paint, colored paper, and pipe cleaners to pull out and keep the children busy while you're doing a task of your own. Add to the craft center with items you and the children collect on your outings (small pebbles, shells, nuts, leaves). And be on the lookout at closeout sales for items that might be used for crafts projects that weren't originally intended for that purpose—buttons, ribbons or wrapping paper, etc.

Clip artist Once your child is old enough to use a pair of scissors, he'll want to practice—on the mail, your favorite magazine, and (watch out) on his own hair. One constructive way to use this new skill is in trimming the coupons mommy has torn out of the Sunday newspaper. Your child will like the feeling of helping, and you'll have a few extra minutes to read the paper.

Growing together If you have houseplants and your child wants to help, let her, but start her with her own plant and her very own, child-size sprinkling can. (The longer the spout, the better.) When she masters her own plant, she can help water the rest—even those hard-to-reach hanging plants, if mommy will hold her.

Finger-lickin' good This is not for a squeamish mom . . . but the kids sure love it. Get a large plate or tray and let your toddler finger paint with something mushy and delicious, like chocolate pudding or whipped cream. You'll have the cleanup problem licked in a minute or two.

Icing on the plate Play with cake-decorating kits, but use mashed potatoes (cheaper and less "junky" than icing). Your child can experiment with the different tips and with colors by using your vegetable dyes.

Artful wrapping Children's artwork can be recycled as gift wrapping rather than discarded. Make sure the artist agrees to this use before you proceed. Artists, like children, may be temperamental.

On the button Sorting, arranging, and otherwise playing with buttons is a great child pastime. But put the buttons on a towel to prevent them from sliding and rolling off the table.

Sectioned off Old egg cartons make ideal disposable mixing trays for paints. Old muffin tins serve the same purpose. They can be used to keep crafts items separate, too.

One person's junk is another person's treasure What's junk mail to you is important mail for your preschooler, who can open it, just like mom and dad.

On a roll Leftover rolls of unprinted newsprint from the newspaper office are inexpensive and can be torn off in large sheets for children to decorate. You're recycling and saving money.

Wipe-off art Take a sheet of Masonite and cover it with clear plastic adhesive. Use the surface for finger painting. If you want a copy of the result, press a clean piece of paper over it. Otherwise, just wipe it off and your child can start again.

Comic transfers To transfer a comic onto a sheet of white paper, mix a teaspoon of dishwashing liquid and one teaspoon of white vinegar. Dab the mixture all over the picture with your finger, then put a piece of white paper over it and rub firmly with the back of a spoon. When you pick up the white paper, you'll see the transfer.

Water painting On warm, sunny days, let your child have a paintbrush and a cup of water to "paint" the house, the sidewalk, etc. There's nothing to clean up.

Go fish First the kids can make the fish—cut them from gallon milk jugs, then glue paper clips on the back. Then they tie a magnet on one end of a string and go fishing.

Bubble trouble Kids love blowing bubbles, but the bubbly commercial liquid that makes them so much fun is slippery stuff. When the bottle gets wet, tiny hands can't quite hold a grip and you get lots of spillage along with tears of disappointment. To prevent this from happening, tape the bottle—while it's still dry—to anything that's handy, a pole, a tree, a pillar on the front porch or a beach umbrella. Make sure it's safely and comfortably within a child's reach. Remember to use waterproof construction tape or electrician's tape.

Climbing fun An eight-foot-long treated landscape timber and two or three short pieces of four-by-four make an inexpensive and effective outdoor balance beam. Treated landscape timber is cheaper than railroad ties, and it comes with rounded edges. Make sure the timber is anchored atop the four-by-four supports. The safest way to anchor it securely is with wooden chocks nailed or screwed into place. Install the screws or nails on the side, so if they ever do come loose, you won't have to worry about children tripping or falling on them.

Cheerio-oh Toddlers seem to like anything that presents them with a simple challenge. One mother strings a length of elastic with Cheerios when she goes to the playground. When it's time for her very active toddler to be put into his stroller, she wipes his hands clean, then presents him with the "necklace" and sits undisturbed while he removes the Cheerios, one by one.

Porcelain palette When your budding little artist begs to express herself in the messiest mediums (finger painting, etc.), let her practice her art in an empty bathtub. When the masterpiece is finished, rinse off the child and rinse down the tub and you've managed to entertain her and complete a cleaning chore, all in one.

Animal behavior A visit to the local pet shop can keep a child amused when you've completely run out of things to do. If you can persuade him that you're at the animal museum (rather than a place where the pets can be bought) you'll have an easier time getting home.

Tents moments Throw a big blanket over the bunk bed or kitchen table and your child has a hideaway. You can also purchase inexpensive tents for indoor or outdoor use. To use where space is at a premium, see if you can buy one of the tents with a bottom surface that fits (like a fitted sheet) over an ordinary mattress and a dome-shaped top that holds its shape with telescoping rods. It makes a wonderful "clubhouse."

Recycling the toys Instead of buying new toys all the time, try bringing out old ones the kids have forgotten about. If you take note of what toys are being used frequently, you can figure out which ignored ones to put aside. Don't bring them out again until the little ones start asking for new toys. What you hope to hear is "Oh, wow! I forgot about those!"

Dress-up play There's not much sense storing this year's Halloween costume in the top of the closet unless you're saving it for a younger sibling. The child probably won't want to be the same character next year anyway. If there's no sibling, put the old costume with other toys for year-round dress-up play. And don't discard *all* your out-of-date clothes (high heels, straw hats, scarves, fedoras, stained flouncy blouses, even old camisoles and half-slips). Set a box of them aside in your child's closet for dress-up play. Then load your camera and allow the box to be "discovered" on a rainy day.

Games Children Play

Even in the days before television, believe it or not, children had a good time. Children who have become accustomed to electronic entertainment, unfortunately, sometimes need to be prodded to find other ways to amuse themselves. But once challenged, they can always rise to the occasion: a child's imagination is a wonderful thing. Try to encourage your child to use it; you will both be astonished at what it can accomplish.

Let's pretend Playacting is a good way for a child to learn to keep busy without the TV. With a beach towel, sunglasses, and a bathing suit a youngster can turn a dreary February day into a glorious summer afternoon. Make a post office, a kitchen, or mommy's or daddy's office.

Free library When it comes to books, very young children know how to rip rather than read. Catalogs and advertising supplements aimed at kids often feature illustrations of *Sesame Street* and other cartoon characters. Instead of throwing them out, present them to your toddler and challenge her: "Can you find Big Bird in here?"

Photo opportunity It's hard to refuse a toddler's request to hold and view photos from the family album, but it's equally hard to stand by and watch the photos be crumpled, smudged, and torn. One mother solved this dilemma by giving her child all the poorly focused, blurred, under- or overdeveloped photos she would normally discard. And baby enjoys showing off "her" photo collection as much as her parents do.

If it feels good, sing it! Don't feel you *must* play traditional games with your children, or sing traditional songs to them. Let the kids play with you—not the other way around. If it's not fun for you, don't do it. If you don't feel comfortable playing peekaboo with your six-month-old, don't. If "Twinkle, Twinkle, Little Star" makes you cringe, don't sing it. One mother told us about a three-year-old who had a repertoire of popular songs under his belt because his dad enjoyed singing them rather than the Mother Goose favorites. As a result, the boy learned to prefer Sinatra and Raffi and was less likely to sing "Mary Had a Little Lamb" than Ray Charles's "Hit the Road, Jack" or 1950s rock and roll.

Wordplay Make up a song using a familiar melody and/or words but substituting names of people you know: for example, John Jacob Grandpa Heimer Schmidt.

Playing alone Some little ones hate having to play alone, even when mommy and daddy have other things to do. One family solved this problem by setting aside a two-hour "Do Your Own Thing" period on weekends. It's not time to spend on idle play. Every activity has a purpose. Parents and child sit down together to draw, paint, read, sew, or simply fold the wash. Children learn by example, and seeing mom and dad enjoying their work or leisure time is a terrific lesson for them. Gradually, they'll initiate their own pastimes.

Different strokes If your in-laws (or spouse, or your own parents) introduce your children to games you find excruciatingly tedious, just tell the child those games are fine, but they're not your favorites. They may continue to play them with granny, dad, or nan but you and they will find other activities.

Author! Author! Kids often have their own ideas of how a story should be told, especially if it's a story that you have been making up as you go along. If your child seems to want to, let her finish the story, or vary the story by having her suggest the topic or start the story while you finish it. No matter how you do it, if you're telling a bedtime story it's always wise to conclude it by having the main character climb into bed after her exhausting adventure is complete. Making your child the star of the story, or patterning the main character after your child in name or appearance, makes the story a lot more fun.

Homemade band instruments A homemade band can consist of maracas (dried beans or buttons in a container that's tightly sealed shut); a guitar (a hole cut in a shoe-box lid, rubber bands slipped around box and lid and over hole); a kazoo (waxed paper attached to one end of an empty toilet-paper or paper-towel roll with a rubber band); cymbals (two pan lids); drum (wooden spoon and pan); and bongos (empty coffee can).

Homemade toys Active minds need more than store-bought toys to keep them busy, and when mom and dad are involved in making the toys, it's family fun. Paste different stickers on one side of poker chips. Toddlers love attempting to match pairs. Older children and adults can play Concentration, first looking at the different stickers, then turning them over and trying to remember which goes with which.

Puppet creations Find "toys" where there are none. Younger children can be easily amused by a sock hand puppet—or even finger hand puppets. Cut off the fingertips of an old glove, and paint on faces. If you're old enough to remember Señor Wences, you can remember how he made a puppet out of a thumb against a clenched fist. Paint eyes on either side of the first knuckle, and move your thumb for the mouth.

Learning tools Kids love pushing buttons and getting reactions, whether it's from a video game or your precious home computer. That's why a used typewriter (manual or electric, depending on the child's age) is both a good investment and a teaching toy for children of all ages. You can often pick one up at a yard sale.

It's a Party!

While one- and two-year-olds barely understand what is going on at a party, by age three a child is quite able to enjoy the proceedings, and by five, may even be something of a host.

Safety in numbers Don't feel obliged to throw an elaborate birthday party for a very young child. A good rule of thumb is to invite the same number of children as the birthday child's age. A small cake and candles plus a few really good pals and presents are more than enough to mark the occasion.

Small appetites No matter how big the cake, remember always to slice and serve child-size portions. But you can announce that seconds are available. There's no sense throwing away enormous amounts of leftovers that are common on most children's plates (yes, even if they're eating dessert). The leftover cake can be frozen in one piece and served as a special dessert.

Gift guidance Before selecting a gift for a child not your own, there are a few general rules to consider. Don't buy anything too big or cumbersome unless you know the parents have plenty of room for big toys. Avoid extravagance, even if you can afford it. Expensive or extravagant gifts just make other parents feel they have to buy expensive presents for your children, too. Toys with many small parts or ones that require complicated assembly ought to be avoided, as well as noisy toys (tin drums, guns with battery-powered or hand-cranked rat-a-tat-tat mechanisms). Clay, finger paints, or anything else that can spill or stain is not a good choice, either, unless a parent approves beforehand.

All for one . . . When ordering custom birthday cakes, get just one big ornament (an edible or inedible flower, clown, or ballerina) and reserve it for the birthday boy or girl. Several different ornaments can start squabbles if they are to be divided or cause resentment if the whole lot is for the birthday child.

And one for all Toddlers usually want exactly what everyone else has, so make sure your party favors or party bags are all the same. Another possibility: have the decorator put flowers in a circular pattern around the cake, making sure there's one for each child.

Holding pattern You don't need the conventional candle holders in a birthday cake. LifeSavers are unusual and pretty. Or you can use gumdrops; just be sure to poke a small hole in each one.

Don't clown around Think twice before hiring a clown (or having a friend dress up as one) for a toddler's party. Some children are terrified of clowns (since they find the makeup and costumes frightening instead of humorous), and a wild-eyed, screaming child can turn the party into a madhouse. If your child insists on having a clown, tell him you have to check with the other mommies first to make sure it's okay. Even then, proceed with caution unless you know for certain none of the guests are clown-aphobes. It takes only one to ruin the day.

Extra, extra If possible, have extras of everything on hand for birthday parties—extra balloons, favors, party bags, plates, cups, and plastic utensils. Balloons pop, cups break, forks get dropped beneath the table, and extra siblings show up unexpectedly.

Party time If you've told the guests to come at noon, and you know the party girl will be on pins and needles for an hour before, tell her you've called the party for 12:15. Guests invariably arrive late, and she'll be delighted to see them "ahead of time" instead of asking every five minutes when they can be expected.

Gift unwrapping When there are lots of children at a birthday party, there are lots of presents. Postpone opening them until after the party. Otherwise, tiny guests may become jealous or restless, and in the confusion of wrapping paper and grabbing hands, it's hard keeping track of who gave what. Waiting until the party is over gives the birthday child something to look forward to after guests have departed and opening presents can be done calmly then. Also you can cull out duplicate gifts and keep boxes intact so they can be passed along or returned. (Make sure you know who gave what, so you don't give the gift back to whoever gave it to your child.) If there are gifts you know your children probably won't ever play with, set them aside discreetly for store returns or future gift giving, too.

Party helpers Here's a hint that covers several areas—it's a timesaver, a money saver, a guide to helping older kids exercise responsibility, and a lesson in how to entertain *lots* of little ones with inexpensive fun and games. When her kindergarten daughter invited the entire class to her birthday celebration, one mother considered hiring an entertainer or a party planner to help. Instead, she hired her ten-year-old son and one of his friends and paid them what to them was a considerable sum but was a fraction of the cost of a professional. The mom also provided detailed instructions of what they were expected to do, how they were to do it, and when. (And of course she remained on hand to supervise.) They helped serve, then shepherded the guests through relay races, pin-the-tail-on-the-donkey, dodge ball, and a host of other games. The five-year-olds loved the party. And the ten-year-olds were proud of a job well done.

In a binder A good stocking stuffer or birthday favor for your child or someone else's: compartmentally divided plastic pages for a three-ring binder meant to hold baseball cards. The individual pockets are good for storing pictures, photos, and other memorabilia.

TV party You may think you have to do something really different for a birthday party, but kids don't. They're very happy to play with their favorite things. Although you may think that kids would find video games, for example, too boring for a birthday entertainment, one mom reports that her older son's favorite party ever was his Nintendo slumber party. His pals brought their games (mom made sure each was labeled), the family borrowed a few television sets and set up several Nintendo "stations," and the kids had the best time—at little cost. For littler ones, watching a familiar videotape at a party is perfectly fine entertainment. As for the menu, again go with the tried and true, like pizza or grilled cheese.

Gifts by the dozen If your small child will be invited to many birthday parties over the course of a year, your best bet is to buy a dozen of one item that will suit all the children. Sometimes you can get a discount, or even a wholesale price, if you order in quantity. Selecting something from a store other than a toy store reduces the chance that everyone else will be giving the same gift. Stationery catalogs sometimes have items—personalized pencils, etc.—that are ideal for this purpose.

Tough Love: Discipline and Rewards

Children need help—some more than others—defining the rules of society. You don't want to stifle them with limits that thwart expression and learning, but you will have anarchy if you give them totally free rein. When you have difficulty laying down the rules, remember that they're actually counting on you for direction and guidance. But don't just tell them when they're behaving incorrectly; they're also looking for you to acknowledge (and reinforce) good behavior.

Close encounters Imagine if your boss, or *your* parents, were twenty feet tall. They'd be talking above you, or down to you, and if they raised their voices, their words would resound like thunder. That's the way it is with little children who aside from their size are still human beings who deserve respect for their feelings and concerns. One smart mom tells us she tries always to see "eye to eye" with her child—even if she doesn't always agree with him. Whenever she needs to get a point across, and to make sure the child understands her, she gets down on her knees, takes his hands in hers, and speaks directly to him. Holding his hands and making eye contact helps the child concentrate and focus his attention. After the discussion, she asks the child to repeat key points, so she knows he has understood what was said. "This technique has *never* failed me," our mother adds.

Don't just say "No" Instead of saying "No!" to your very young child all the time, try saying "uh-oh" and changing your tone of voice as the occasion warrants it. You'll sound more like a cautioning parent than a negative one.

We're keeping an eye on you A photo of mom, dad, grandma, or any favorite adult in the playroom suggests a grown-up presence while a parent is busy elsewhere in the house.

Purposeful play Introducing a child to new situations or getting her to go along with certain routines that may not rank high as entertainment may go more smoothly if you act out acceptable behavior with some of her favorite toy characters—dolls, stuffed animals, or cartoon figures. Go through the situation or routine (diaper change, haircut, meal at table, doctor's examination, sitting quietly in church) and let the child participate. Once kids have a sense of control over things, especially occasions that may initially seem strange or frightening to them, they tend to be much more cooperative.

Bribery—or reward? There's a fine line between bribing a child and giving rewards for good behavior. If the reward is offered before the child has performed the task expected, is that bribery? It depends on the circumstances. More than one parent swears that a system of rewards makes toilet training, going to bed alone, first haircuts, sibling arrivals—almost anything that requires a behavioral transition—much easier and they don't care whether it's offered before or after compliance. Other parents warn against succumbing to "outright bribery," so that a child eventually demands a reward every time she fulfills a simple request. Once that happens, you're both in trouble. Which way to go probably depends on the personality of your child.

All washed up Children seem to be inherently indisposed to the idea of washing their hands. Instead of having a quarrel about it, ask the child to wash something, such as a toy. Hands are washed in the process and there's no parental challenge involved.

Beat the clock Kitchen timers are great for instilling a sense of time in kids. Use them when your child wants your attention but you can't leave what you're doing. Just set the timer and tell the child he has X number of minutes to finish cleaning his room, or reading, or playing, before you can join him. Remember to put the timer where he is to give him the opportunity to remind you. It makes him feel *so* important.

Better than "No" Three magic words that keep twenty-month-old-plus babies happy when they insist on doing something or eating something that doesn't fit your schedule are "later," "tomorrow," or "next time." A toddler's memory bank isn't very efficient, and putting it off is gentler than just saying "No."

Hands off When active preschoolers fight, tell them to "use words, not hands" to express themselves. It sounds awfully simple, but that's how children learn the difference between constructive behavior and destructive behavior, a lesson they'll need in order to get along with others for the rest of their lives.

Govern, don't rule Another example of teaching by example: When children get too loud or rambunctious at play, or when the occasional tantrum takes hold, that's the time for parents to hold *their* tongues and tempers. Lower your voice, don't raise it. Call "time-out" with the dignity and gravity of a story-book butler. Children will respond seriously if the occasion demands it, and of course many potential occasions present themselves.

Just one touch Encouraging young children to say "Excuse me" before they interrupt a conversation can backfire when they start abusing the privilege and subject you to a constant barrage of "Excuse me"s. It's an attention getter that can drive older siblings crazy, too, especially during meals or at story-telling time. To avoid the problem, tell your child that when she feels she absolutely has to get your attention right away she should gently touch your arm with her hand and leave it there. Make sure she understands that's a silent signal that will tell you that she has a question and she will be acknowledged, but she has to wait until you finish your conversation, your sentence, paragraph, or page before you will turn to her. Perhaps a nod or a brief "I'll be right with you"—some sign that you've gotten her signal—will help her be patient.

Less is more Nothing gets a child's attention faster than whispering whatever it is you want to say. This is a trick that adults can use in dealing with other adults, too: lowering (instead of raising) your voice makes people strain to pay attention and they focus on the message more completely.

The last word's the only one you'll need While watching a talk show, one mother had a revelation that she tells us changed her whole approach to child rearing and discipline. The guest, a child psychologist, mentioned that the chief complaint he received from parents was having to tell their children something 1,000 times before they'd listen. "*That's* the problem," the psychologist said. "Parents tell their kids to do something 999 times too many." Something clicked, and this particular mother vowed to follow the doctor's advice. It was rough going at first, she reports. "We were on our way to a party we were all looking forward to, and the kids were fighting in the backseat. I told them to settle down and if they didn't stop we would turn around and go home. I told them that was their only warning. They totally ignored me so we went home. We missed a few more outings over the next few weeks but they soon got the message. Now, when I talk, they listen, and I only have to say it once."

The bad boys' club When discipline is called for, don't label your child a "bad boy" or "naughty girl." Labels leave a bitter taste, teach nothing, and may even backfire. If a child is convinced of his intrinsic badness, why should he even attempt to be good? Remember, it's not your child who needs correcting (you know your child is perfect)—it's the child's behavior. And that's the message to convey: "You're not behaving very well and you're the only one who can fix your behavior, so please change it!" You'll be surprised by how well children respond to such "straight talk."

Price controls Before you get to the store on a day when you have promised to buy a treat, designate a price limit. This is not only helpful to the child but to you, since you may find yourself spending more than you had planned if the hassling wears you down.

Sweet talk How do you teach children that they may be more successful asking for something quietly rather than demanding it loudly? One parent devised a Wake Up Game. Daddy pretends he's fallen asleep, and Mommy says, "Let's try to wake him up." Then the whole family yells together. "Daddy! Wake up." But shouting at daddy doesn't seem to work. Mother says, a second time. "Let's try whispering." And everyone whispers quietly. "Daddy . . . It's time to get up." That does the trick. The lesson that is pointed out, of course, is that speaking softly does the job. (The lesson about carrying a big stick can be learned later.)

Wants and whys Some of the things children want have little relationship to the child's true desire. Getting to the underlying message requires understanding and patience. So often, parents fail to explore the reasons behind the want, especially when it sounds unreasonable. A classic example is the case of a mother whose five-year-old son began asking, day after day, when the family was going to go camping again. At first, his mother could only think to remind him that camping was a once-a-year affair. After a few days of his asking, she asked why he was in such a hurry to camp out again. "So we can have barbecued chicken," he replied. It wasn't the event he was hungering for, just the main course.

Avoiding the hassle If a child asks for a new toy for himself every time you enter a toy store to buy a birthday gift for someone else, it's a lot easier to say, "Let's put it on our list," than just to say no. Although evasion is not as effective as direct confrontation with an older child, with a young one it may make sense. Often the object desired is just a whim of the moment and being suckered into a long conversation about it isn't worth your time.

Mother's little helper Her four-year-old daughter was prone to whining and tantrums until this mother gave the child a job to do. Giving three- to five-year-olds some simple chore to perform helps build their self-esteem and provides an occasion for well-deserved praise.

Sweet tooth solution Halloween brings candy—loads of it—and even kids who don't normally have a sweet tooth want to eat it *all,* as if gorging were part of the ritual. One mother solved this problem by letting her four-year-old son pick ten items from his Halloween hoard that he could eat over the next week. But what about the rest of it? Throwing it away seemed wasteful, so a deal was cut whereby he could sell the remainder to his mom for a fair price and buy a small toy with the proceeds. And the leftovers? Send them to a charity or take them to mom's or dad's office for distribution.

Taking ten Instead of harping about how everyone in the house always leaves shoes, clothes, toys lying around, take a ten-minute cleanup break when the spirit moves you. Make sure everyone (including dad) has a job, and stick to the time limit. If any member of the family finishes early, the next job is to cheer the others on to completion. Don't overdo it. Just take ten minutes, but do it as often as you feel it's necessary. The family will either get the message and start picking up as soon they take things off, or they'll look forward to some family fun and togetherness by doing it as a group. Either way, you're all winners.

Working together Want to teach good habits by example? When it comes to cleaning your child's room, offer to do it together—so long as your requirements are made clear to your child and you don't wind up doing all the work. Once the assignments have been split and delegated, the two of you may even have fun while cleaning.

Hold for the count It's hard sometimes for children to make the transition from one activity to another. When it's time to get into the stroller and go, or share a toy, or separate from a parent in the morning, the sudden change can set off a panicked response, caused by fear, wounded pride, plain stubbornness, or a legitimate inability to cope. One mother uses this trick to give the child time to adjust: "*After* I've counted to ten, you'll . . ." It's amazing how little it takes to ease the transition, she reports. The child may see it as a face-saving measure, or it may simply give her time to adjust her behavior.

Just looking, thanks Another way to avoid arguments about whether or not the time is appropriate to shop for toys (or anything else a child demands during a shopping trip) is to designate special Buying Days and Looking Days. Make sure an understanding is reached on which kind of day it is before you leave the house. This prevents constant arguments and negotiations, particularly if you are at a toy store buying a gift for another child.

A day at a time One mother established candy day once a week and made a big deal of going out and choosing a candy bar with her child. Instead of saying no all the time, she could say, "Yes, you can have that candy bar on candy bar day." Your child may prefer to celebrate soda day or ice-cream day.

Prochoice Kids, even preschoolers, love making their own decisions. Choosing builds confidence and provides them with a degree of independence. The trick is to offer choices where either answer is acceptable to you. "Which do you want to do first, brush your teeth or put on pajamas?" The same holds true for getting dressed. "Which socks, the white ones or the blue ones?" Agree on two outfits the night before. Next day, ask: "Which outfit? This one or that one?" Offering a child too many choices can be time-consuming and frustrating, while offering limited choices is the ideal compromise and helps the child build his or her ego.

A show of appreciation After walking in and finding her five-year-old son quietly reading in bed one morning, his delighted mother went to the kitchen, cooked his favorite breakfast, and served it to him in bed. "You know what this is for" was all she said. The boy was thrilled: he recognized the treat as an incentive to do more reading, and he did.

Good times Once a day, and particularly when you're having a hard day, review all the good things the child has done that day, even if it's nothing more than putting a shirt on correctly. Your child will love you for noticing how well she did.

Fighting and Sharing

One of the most important things your child will learn in nursery school is how to share, so if your very small child hasn't yet gotten the message, don't be concerned. Children at this age may not understand the concept of sharing, so minimize the opportunities for disputes. Don't expect any child to learn the concept of sharing overnight. You have to keep plugging away at it, trying new methods until the message sinks in. *Don't give up and don't give in.* Sharing and learning to play go hand in hand. You're doing your child a big favor by insisting, whenever the occasion calls for it, that she's capable of being part of a team, which is what sharing is all about. She'll have plenty of time to play on her own, with only her imagination for company. As they get older, of course, children continue to improve in their ability to get along with friends in school and play situations, but sibling rivalry seems to go on forever. Helping children get along with others, and particularly with brothers and sisters, is a major playground topic.

Sibling day Some parents feel it's unfair to give older or younger children a gift on a sibling's birthday, reasoning that they'll get their special day soon enough. Others like the idea, seeing it as a way to defuse sibling jealousy at birthdays. If you lean toward the latter solution, try this variation on the theme: Inaugurate a private, family-only "sister's day" or "brother's day" to coincide with the main event. Let the birthday child present the sibling with a small gift to commemorate the day he or she became one. Both children give and receive, and the sibling doesn't feel empty-handed. Or let the sibling also have a special friend over during the party as a distraction and to enable you to concentrate on party fun. If the older sibs are old enough, hire them to help out.

Red is me, blue is you Tired of hearing: "That's mine!" "No, it's mine!"? One way to resolve the problems—even with pre-readers—is to color-code possessions. If one child is red and another is blue, you can keep track of everything from toothbrushes to game pieces. You can either buy items in the child's special color or use markers or stickers to flag them. (Avoid picking hard-to-find hues if you want to be able to find items in his or her colors.)

Mirror images If children are fighting, give them each a rag sprayed with window cleaner, position them in front of a mirror and ask them to clean it. As they look in the mirror, the giggles will eventually take over. You can also work this with two children at one window—one standing on the porch outside, one inside.

Color wars When children are fighting over toys, ask each child to pick a color and then to help you separate the toys into color groups. Each child may play with toys of his or her color only. Not only does that solve the argument, but children soon tire of being restricted and generally agree to share on their own.

Fair share Whenever there is something to divide in order to share, make it a policy that whoever does the dividing must allow the other to choose first. Even Solomon couldn't have worked this out better. You will never see a fight about who got the larger piece since the one who makes the split is extra-special cautious about seeing that both halves are exactly equal.

Toy sharing Many parents have recommended setting aside certain toys for "sharing." Sharing toys are kept in a special place or container. One mother has taken the idea a step further. She turned one room of her house into a "sharing room." Any toy that strays into the room must be shared with others.

Polite pairing Try to have two identical sets of crayons, coloring books, and inexpensive puzzles on hand for play dates. It eliminates the need for lectures on sharing and frees the time for fun.

Dividing the responsibility Another way to encourage sharing is to ask the parent or baby-sitter of the visiting playmate to bring a "sharing toy" or two along so your child won't have sole responsibility for the sharing process.

Just for you Fights over who gets to play with what toy can be avoided by having a special basket of toys reserved for playmates. Let your own child select the toys for the visitor's basket, and let her change them at will—so long as the changes are made before the visitor arrives. Very young children may not understand the concept of "What's yours is yours and mine is mine," but older ones may be able to go along with this plan.

To share or not to share One way to solve the sharing problem is to remove the toys that your child considers special. Have your child select the toys she *doesn't* want to share before a friend comes over for a play date. Put those toys away, out of mind and out of reach of both the children.

Bully idea If a child starts behaving like a bully in nursery school or at a day-care center, ask the teacher to put him in with a group of older, bigger children for a few days. He'll realize there are limits to his bullying behavior, and when he returns to his own age group, he'll generally be much less aggressive.

Taking turns A mother writes: "My kids are very competitive with each other so we started a system of odd-even days. On my son's day, he brushes his teeth first, gets the favorite red cup, picks his story first. This routine has solved a very difficult problem of remembering who got the red cup yesterday or who was read to first. During those six times of the year when the odd days come together, 31st and 1st, we do a 'sharing day,' when they have to work things out. Eventually, the system will phase out so that the kids can work things out themselves. But for now, and especially since they are so close in age and so highly competitive owing to this closeness, we use what works."

What does the contract say? In any negotiation, you're better off when the terms of the arrangement are written down. The same goes for the deals you make with your kids. Spell out your arrangements (and post a copy, if the child is old enough to read). This can apply to anything from the arrangement for the allowance (and under what terms money can be withheld) to the specifics of what chores must be done.

Equal time Fights over how long the other child had a toy can be avoided if you use a timer. Each is allotted equal time.

Agreeing to agree When there's a verbal agreement, the parties are more likely to end up in court than if there's a written one. If a "time-out" rule is proposed in your house, the first time-out should be for a meeting of the minds. You and the kids compile a list of time-out offenses and write them down. Post them in a conspicuous spot. When a fight starts, time-out takes on real meaning. This is a learning skill as well.

Fighting: calling time-out Putting time-out in a real time frame is a great way to cool down a rumpus, especially when three or four kids are involved. Use a kitchen timer and set it according to the age of the offender—three minutes for three-year-olds, four minutes for four-year-olds, etc. A good way to develop a sense of time in kids, too!

Table games When kids start teasing each other at the dinner table, reprimanding them can be counterproductive. ("Well, he started it!" "Did not!" "Did so!") Switch gears instead, and divert their attention. "Let's play Simon Says: Simon says put your hands on your head . . . Simon says pick up your fork . . . Eat your dinner! I didn't say Simon says! Now—Simon says eat your dinner."

Shelf-ishness Giving each of your children a special shelf or toy box can cut down endless sibling fighting over toys. Any toy on his shelf or in her box is off limits to others. *Any toys not being played with that are lying around and not put back on the shelf are wild—they may be chosen by anyone.* This excellent tip not only stops arguments but helps keep kids' rooms tidy.

Trade-ins Two-year-olds know exactly what "mine!" means, but they have trouble understanding "sharing." Two-year-olds often equate sharing with a loss of power, especially when there's a new baby in the house. In order to encourage older siblings to share, try "trading in" their old toys. Whenever the older child gets a new toy, or book, or game, tell him he has to trade in one he's tired of or outgrown, preferably so it can be handed down.

It's my turn! When there are more than two kids in the family, there's only one fair way to settle arguments about whose turn it is to sit next to the window or the jukebox in the diner, who gets the front seat in the car, and who pays the toll or gets the prize in the cereal box, etc., *Keep a list.* It works because it establishes proof, and kids love to see things *proved.* Just keep a pen and a notebook or a few scraps of paper handy at all times.

Learning to Help

A very small child is eager to help, regarding it as a privilege. It's only as the child grows that he begins to regard it as a burden. What helps is if the helping is required and expected as a matter of course, not introduced and imposed as a punishment. If you don't want to feel resentful and imposed upon, take it upon yourself to train your helpers, starting as young as possible. Even very small children can perform simple tasks if the parents are creative about it, and as the child's skills improve he is of genuine help.

Full employment Kids love the thought of doing jobs for parents—exercising responsibilities and having control over things—but there's a big gap between thought and expression for a two-year-old. Simple tasks at which they can't fail are best. Here are chores even a two-year-old can take seriously: delivering baby's diapers to the hamper, carrying mail and newspapers into the house, and shutting off the lights in her room before bedtime.

Coupon cutting Children old enough to use a pair of scissors can be encouraged to go through the Sunday newspaper cutting out coupons for items the family uses regularly. As a treat, they may be allowed to select one or two items they would like to try.

At child level Once they're past the babyproofing stage, you can encourage your children to open the cabinets that are easy to reach. Put napkins, plates, and cups at that level so your child can help set the table or help herself to items she may need at snack time.

Supermarket scavenging On market day, take the coupons you have clipped (perhaps with the help of your child) and tell your child you're going on a scavenger hunt in the market. Organize the coupons by aisle, and as you start down each one, give her the food items to be found in that aisle and ask her to hunt for them. This task eliminates restlessness and tantrums, keeps the child from running off, and promotes learning. You save some money, too.

A mommy's little sherpa Little kids (two to five) see bigger kids carrying backpacks, so why not let them feel grown-up by giving them pint-sized backpacks of their own. In fact, these will be of real use: small backpacks are just big enough to carry the things you'd normally put into your diaper bag. They look cute, the idea is practical, and the sooner kids learn how to hold—and tote—their own, the better.

The Waiting Game

The passage of time is a hard concept for young children to absorb. Youngsters who seem very sophisticated in language skills still sometimes have difficulty understanding how far away the day after tomorrow can be. Learning how to wait for anything—ten minutes for dessert, two hours until we leave for the beach, two weeks for a special occasion or until mom and dad come back from a trip away—is a real challenge. The more concrete mom and dad can make these concepts seem, the easier for a child.

Making time fly If mommy and/or daddy have to go away for extended periods of time (business travel, vacation), here's a clever way to help children count the days before a parent returns without raising their anxiety level. Staple together a stack of small scraps of paper, the number of pages to be determined by the number of days you'll be gone. Each scrap contains a clue as to where a special surprise is hidden, or names a special treat for that day (dessert, video rental, etc.). Whoever is in charge of minding the children keeps the stack in a safe place (no peeking!) and announces how many slips and surprises are left. You'll know it works when the kids begin suggesting you take longer trips.

Advance notice A child's "sense of time" is a misnomer. Their internal clocks are most often tuned to their digestive systems, rather than the cerebral cortex. Even the brightest three-year-old has trouble understanding the difference between a day and a week. For all those reasons, it's never a good idea to tell young children about an exciting forthcoming event more than two days in advance. The anticipation can be unbearable for them, and repeated cries of "When are we going to the circus (or grandma's)?" can be hard on your nerves, too.

Teaching time Since the concept of time—yesterday, tomorrow, next week—comes so slowly, it is very difficult for a young child to learn how to anticipate an event that's a week or two (or more) away. In one Scottish town, children are told to count the number of "sleeps" leading up to an event, such as the arrival of a visitor or return of a parent. It's an easier concept for a child to grasp than the number of days. If the wait is a matter of minutes or hours, use TV shows as a gauge. Explaining that "We'll be there in two *Sesame Streets*" may actually inspire some patience.

Keeping track While you're away, homemade calendars are wonderful ways to let little ones know you care. Counting the days seems to make time fly and gives children a tangible expression of your absence. Boxes labeled with the days you're away can be filled in daily by the children. Some children enjoy pasting a numbered sticker in the box as each day ends or inserting a numbered tab into a slot. "Secret doors" (a simple flap) concealing a special message can also be opened one day at a time. This tip is ideal for young ones just learning numbers, too.

Children's savings time Celebrating New Year's Eve with young children ("Please let us stay up!") can result in youngsters who are cranky and overtired by the time the ball drops. Try this instead: Slowly set the clocks forward to midnight—when the children are not in the room. Compress three or four hours into one, and don't let them catch you at it! Though the time may really be 8:45 P.M., the kids believe it's a quarter to midnight, and within 20 minutes are willing to be tucked in and ready for sleep.

When mom and dad are away Children love surprises, especially after prolonged absences from either parent. But why wait until you return home from a trip to present the surprise? Gather some manila envelopes, and date them for each day you'll be away. Put in them a special treat, candy, a photo, or a little trinket. Set aside a special time during the day when "mommy mail" or "daddy mail" can be opened. Kids love this idea, and the time parents are away seems to fly by faster.

Travelogue Kids ought to know where their parents go and what they do when they travel on business. A short videotape of mom or dad standing in front of a familiar landmark and telling their children they miss them and think of them all the time is a nice surprise when kids start asking when daddy or mommy is coming home.

Trip books If mom or dad has to go away on a trip or if the child is going with one parent only on a trip, make a book using photographs of the child and the absent parent. Make a montage with magazine cutouts showing the mode of transportation (plane, car) and a story about the trip from a child's point of view. Great for very young children, one to three.

The Parent-Teacher

As a parent, you spend a tremendous amount of your time teaching—not just by example, but also directly. You teach your child what to expect of life, and you teach your child what life expects of him. You teach everything from minding Ps and Qs to understanding the ABCs. Although parents have many different tips for helping their child learn, there is a thread that runs through so many of them it's worth noting. That thread is to wait for opportunities when children seem eager to learn rather than forcing information on them. When they're ready they will be more receptive.

Literary shortcut When a little one is ready to start writing her own name but can't, cut out a stencil of it and let her fill in the space with crayon, pencil, or pen. Encourage her to do it in as few strokes as necessary, and she'll soon be forming letters with no help from you or from the stencil.

Money supersavers We think this is the best idea we've seen for teaching children the value of savings and how to manage money. Start when they're as young as four by tying their allowance to a saving system in which you're the banker. Get yourself a small account book and observe these simple rules: (1) Whatever the amount you decide, the child's weekly allowance is guaranteed, not tied to good or bad behavior, chores, or grades. (2) Allowance (all or part) can be spent or saved; if saved, parents will match the amount and a record will be kept. (3) Withdrawals must be discussed with parents and can never exceed half the amount in the account. All entries are made in front of the child at a set time each week. This system can go on until the child is ready for his own bank account.

Safety in numbers When a child begins learning to count and memorize the ABCs, that's the time to teach him your address and phone number as well. It could make a big difference if he ever gets lost or strays off during a school outing or a trip with a baby-sitter.

Spellbound In order to settle down a precocious four-year-old, who was still posing interesting questions at bedtime—after bath and story-book reading—her parents played to the child's eagerness to learn instead of fighting it. After reading time was over, they turned to vocabulary building. A new, "secret" word was selected every night and written down in a special note-book. The child read it back, learning spelling and pronunciation and associating it with happy family times.

Toddler trivia Ever have trouble telling the difference between *Sesame Street*'s Bert and Ernie? Just remember that *B*ert is the one who looks like a *b*anana.

Money-making lists and saving up Sitting down with a child and making a list of things he wants but you might not be able to afford at present (Nintendos, motorcycles, expensive sneakers) is a good way to avoid having to say "No" without limiting discussion. Looking at a list of items and seeing how fast it grows (and how it changes!) can be a positive learning experience that helps a child focus realistically on what he can have and when he can have it. Let him freely add (or subtract) things to (or from) the list and he'll start exercising discretion.

Playing the fool When April Fool's Day rolls around, don't play tricks on children, no matter what their age. A child will often interpret an April Fool trick as a betrayal of trust, not a laugh riot. Tears are just one result; the emotional hurt cuts deeper. If there's to be a joke—let it be on you.

Changes and Moves

Even adults have a difficult time dealing with changes and transitions. But as an adult, you at least have some control over the situation. A child, on the other hand, is pretty much at the mercy of others and often doesn't understand either the purpose of changes or what the consequences can be. Parents can minimize the traumatic effect of anything from the first day of school to the first day in a new house by helping the child prepare for it as gradually as possible.

Getting one's bearings First-time events such as the first haircut or the first day of school always go smoother when parent and child have something to refer to and talk about. Start with *Berenstain Bears* and *Mister Rogers,* but any book or poem or story that relates to the event is a jumping-off point that lets the child know it's only the first time for him.

School plans Some popular nursery schools accept applications as much as a year in advance. Check with any school you're considering, or may be considering, to find out whatever you need to know—from tuition costs to application procedures to hours.

Meet the classmates The summer before your child starts preschool or nursery school, get the class list and set up play dates so the children won't be complete strangers to each other when school starts. It makes the children's transition so much easier, and you'll be surprised how much it means to parents and teachers.

Marking the way If you will be walking your child to school, plan a route together in advance. You can pick out landmarks such as stores, street signs, buildings, etc. to "greet" each day. Before school actually starts, walk the route a few times to rehearse it. By the time school starts, the walk will be a comforting and familiar ritual.

Visiting the school If your child is especially wary about the first day of school, it might not be enough to introduce him to the teacher beforehand. So let him see how the school works—from the kitchen to the administrative offices. A short tour will familiarize him with his new surroundings and help conquer his fear of strangers.

Moving plan Moving to a new house or town need not be stressful for children if some precautions are taken. Start with a reading of the Berenstain Bears' *Moving Day* and follow up with a discussion of the events described in the book. Visit the new house or show the child lots of pictures of not just the house but the local park, market, toy store, school, even hospital. Kids want to know that everything will be there. Spare the child the sight of items being discarded or given away, since this "letting go" may be upsetting.

Friends new and old What makes a new place to live seem familiar, in addition to personal possessions, is of course the sight of a friendly face. If your child is assured there will be playmates in new surroundings, he'll be much less apprehensive about a move, so if possible try to find an acquaintance your child's age and arrange for a play date. Your new school can supply you with a list of names. In the best of all situations, you can also invite old friends to the new house right away, so your child will realize that moving doesn't always mean giving up old friendships. As for friends left behind, if children are too young to write letters to one another, how about exchanging hellos on a videotape?

A room of their own The transition won't be so wrenching if children have a part in the planning, so involve your child in decorating the new room. Look at color charts together, for example, and allow your child to select some new decorative piece, such as a picture frame or mirror or bulletin board. But don't forget that the old things are also reassuring, so make the point that the old, familiar toys will be brought along, as will pets and other beloved possessions. To make this point more strongly, if you will be able to visit the new house with the children, have them bring along some toys to leave there.

Where are my things? To ease the trauma of moving into a new home, allow each child to pack one special box with favorite things. Make sure this box is clearly labeled (if they're old enough, children can label the boxes themselves), and make sure those boxes are the last to be loaded and the first to be unloaded. It keeps kids busy and takes their minds off the place they're departing from, and gives them something familiar to look forward to upon arrival.

Establishing your own traditions Particularly if the family has to cope with physical moves, it's important to have traditions to give children a sense of security and comfort. Fortunately, it's not hard to establish a tradition. Do something special more than once with your children and you're on the way to establishing a ritual. It can be as grand as going to the same place for vacation each year, or as simple as serving dad's special apple pancakes or mom's French toast on Sunday mornings. Childhood memories *and* adult dreams spring from sources such as these. Years ago, when life was less complicated, families did everything together. Nowadays, gatherings that include the whole family are less frequent but just as meaningful. But these memorable occasions won't happen by themselves. They need planning. And that can be one of the most important and creative aspects of parenting.

Index

Index

Index

Index

Index

Index

Index

Index